In My
FATHER'S
Garden

In My

FATHER'S

Garden

A DAUGHTER'S

SEARCH FOR A

SPIRITUAL LIFE

Kim Chernin

Algonquin Books of Chapel Hill   1996

Published by
ALGONQUIN BOOKS OF CHAPEL HILL
Post Office Box 2225
Chapel Hill, North Carolina 27515-2225

a division of
WORKMAN PUBLISHING
708 Broadway
New York, New York 10003

LIBRARY OF CONGRESS CATALOGING-IN-PUBLICATION DATA
Chernin, Kim.

    In my father's garden : a daughter's search for a spiritual life /
Kim Chernin.

        p.   cm.
    ISBN 1-56512-100-7

    1. Chernin, Kim—Family.   2. Women authors, American—
20th century—Family relationships.   3. Fathers and daughters—
United States—Biography.   4. Spiritual life.   I. Title.
PS3553.H3558Z466   1996
813'.54—dc20
[B]   96-10377
                                                               CIP

10   9   8   7   6   5   4   3   2   1
First Edition

For

My Father

Paul Kusnitz

(1900–1967)

and

My Mother

Rose Chernin

(1901–1995)

and

My Friend

Diane Cleaver

(1943–1995)

Contents

I am done with great things and big plans, great institutions and big success. I am for those tiny, invisible loving human forces that work from individual to individual, creeping through the crannies of the world like so many rootlets, or like the capillary oozing of water, which, if given time, will rend the hardest monuments of pride.

—William James

In My
FATHER'S
Garden

Prologue

IN THE SHADOW OF
A FALLING FLOWER

*M*y father had a garden, flourishing in full view in our backyard. But his garden might as well have been sealed away in thorny, fairytale terrain. I was my mother's daughter, and since that is what I was meant to be, I managed not to take in the potency of my father's garden or the meaning of the work he did there, although he was working in the garden every Saturday and Sunday and on most summer evenings, after he and I had washed the dinner dishes.

I was my mother's daughter—stormy, revolutionary, a person you might find at a barricade. In our house (and it was in every sense my mother's house), we held meetings, read newspapers, watched the news. We folded leaflets on the dining room table after the evening meal was cleared, stamped and addressed envelopes, debated Marxism, and discussed foreign events. Our telephone had a regular place at the dinner table, where my mother, a political organizer, seemed always to receive emergency calls. In the mornings I would see her drag the long cord around the kitchen, the phone tucked into her shoulder as she gave instructions and made tactical plans while preparing our meal.

I have told many stories about my mother's house. My father's garden was always missing from them. I always knew how much I had been molded by my mother's stormy temperament, but I was not able to trace back to my father's garden any traits of heart, mind, or spirit that might have grown up in me.

A garden is a place where a sense of kinship with nature or with a force larger than oneself is easily encountered. There is no need to weed these intimations out or fit them into the pattern of more formal ideologies. These dream thoughts can soon be closed away in the shed along with the trowel and rake. I mean the kind of thought your hands think, digging a hole. The sort of idea your knees get while you are putting a seed in the earth. Thoughts held in the shadow of a falling flower or slipped off like a pair of canvas gardening gloves after a day's hard work. The kind of thoughts that were not welcome in my mother's house.

There, we planned to shake things up. We thought we

could change the way the world had been for a long time. We valued action in the name of the collective, we stood for comradely dedication, disciplined freedom of choice.

My father's garden was a more subtle and subversive place. Out there, my father seemed interested in the natural laws to which one adapts oneself, the kind of intelligence that allows grass seed to grow grass, cherry stones to ripen cherries. In a garden one learns about what is likely to come again. One practices the patience to wait for earthy resurrections and to perform the small, hard work that makes for an abundant crop.

Every family passes down a legacy, a characteristic way of putting children to bed at night, telling its stories, interpreting the world. In my family there was a divided legacy, one part flourishing above ground, the other cautious and subterranean. If both legacies had been declared, they would have been at war, the values of the house trooping out to put down the virtues of the garden. But my father's garden would never have invaded my mother's house.

Gardens have an odd way of growing inward when you think they have been left outside. As I grow older, I find that my father's garden has taken root in me, that I am perhaps my father's gentle, dreamy child even more than I had been my mother's tempestuous daughter. With this discovery, I am faced with a new task and must set about to make peace between my mother's militancy and my father's love for an hour's contemplative work. This is the task I have inherited, although neither of my parents could have known it.

I AM ABOUT to think some thoughts that come right out of my father's garden, thoughts that would have been unthinkable in my mother's house. Therefore, because I need help, I am going to turn to William James, an American pragmatic philosopher who was not afraid of unthinkable thoughts:

> Were one asked to characterize the life of religion in the broadest and most general terms possible, one might say that it consists of the belief that there is an unseen order, and that our supreme good lies in harmoniously adjusting ourselves thereto. This belief and this adjustment are the religious attitude of the soul.

What does this have to do with me, a stock late-twentieth-century unbeliever? In the years since I left my mother's house, I had gone along into the bleak, intellectually fashionable mode of believing in nothing. I had studied Marx, Jung, Freud, and feminism, hoping each would explain the mysteries of human destiny, clarify uncertainties about why we are set down here on this planet in the way we are. In time, I had grown adjusted to my progressive disillusionment. It was, I supposed, dignified, even heroic to live one's life without systematic truths. Maybe that is what maturity means—believing in nothing, getting on with one's life against a muffled questioning about why one bothers. Working hard, devoting oneself to friends and family, keeping a solemn eye on death, the interrupter. It would take a hell of a jolt to shake someone in this state into another possibility of experiencing the world.

This is what happened to me. It happened in the garden. This experience unearthed a deep-rooted belief in an unseen order. Through this belief I hope to bring about a reconciliation between my father's garden and my mother's house.

James has interesting remarks to make about this as well:

Our ordinary alterations of character, as we pass from one of our aims to another, are not commonly called transformations, because each of them is so rapidly succeeded by another in the reverse direction; but whenever one aim grows so stable as to expel definitively its previous rivals from the individual's life, we tend to speak of the phenomenon, and perhaps to wonder at it, as a "transformation."

I used to think people on spiritual paths were world-withdrawers, lurking about in melancholy woodland places. They were the incense burners, the chanters, the shavers of heads, the meditators. But what if the spiritual path leads one not away from but right back into the world, with a renewed sense of vigor for amending it? Amending the world, fixing it up, saving it from itself: these are the ideas that were at home in my mother's house. It never occurred to me (it would have been a forbidden, heretical idea) that spiritual people might be comrades in this endeavor.

SO WHO AM I now that I have taken on this task of reconciliation? I live with a woman I love, in the Berkeley Hills. She has planted a garden with white roses, enormous dahlias, passionflowers growing into the neighbor's trees.

We have a house with a view of San Francisco, the Golden Gate Bridge, Mount Tamalpais. The floors of our house are made out of bubinga, a dark red West African wood. We write in the mornings. We speak with people in the afternoons. Many of them are women who are troubled about their lives. Some of these people are interested in a spiritual life, some have been what they call spiritual since childhood.

The basic structure of my life (house and home, partner, listening to people who come to talk about their lives) has remained unchanged for many years, as has my writing schedule. I take walks in the woods, listen to opera, especially when sung by Maria Callas, Catherine Malfitano, Kirsten Flagstad, and Cecilia Bartoli. Listening to music used to be the way I worshiped; reading poetry was a form of prayer.

Emily Dickinson wrote, "There is a certain slant of light on winter afternoons that oppresses with the heft of cathedral tunes. A heavenly hurt it gives us, we can find no scar but internal difference where the meanings are."

Everything about these lines matches up with my own recent experience in the garden: the slant of light, the anguish it brings with it, the internal difference where the meanings are. Emily too had her transformations. One of her old school chums described her as "exquisitely neat and careful in her dress . . . [She] always had flowers about her. She was one of the wits of the school, and there were no signs in her life and character of the future recluse." Eventually, she ended up wandering about the garden of her father's house with her dog Carlo. She baked bread for the family, watching village life from her window. When she saw the chestnut tree in bloom she thought the skies were in blossom. Some people say she was in love with her sister-in-law Sue Dickinson, who lived next door. I can imagine she loved Sue and also that she was a passionate lover of the mystic's god, although in conventional terms she was not a believer.

Of her family she wrote: "They are religious, except me, and address an eclipse, every morning, whom they call their 'Father.'" She was, however, familiar with a "noiseless noise" in the orchard and knew a great deal about ecstasy: "Come slowly Eden," she instructed. "Lips unused to thee, Bashful, sip thy jasmines, As the fainting bee." I would say she knew what she needed to know about the world's unseen order, in the intimate immediate sense in which Saint Theresa also knew, as did Hildegard von Bingen, the medieval nun whose devotional poems and music have recently become popular again.

What do these women have to do with me? I probably hope, through them, to smuggle out a declaration of my own mystical learnings, as if I cannot get used to the idea that I take my lineage from my father's garden, and do not have to be apologetic about this when my mother stands gazing out at me from the door of her house.

HOW DID IT all begin, this fascination with gardens and the hidden nature of my father? I was worried about the world. Even on a good day I am a worrier. Out for a walk on a cold winter night, it would suddenly occur to me, there are people down on Telegraph Avenue who are living on the street and I sure wouldn't like to be sleeping outdoors on a cold night like this. Another day, I worried about the ozone layer, the disappearance of frogs from the hills up near our house, the discovery of lead-contaminated soil down by the bay when they were building the new freeway, the little girl who got shot by a drug dealer in her own neighborhood. I saw her running across the front page of our local newspaper. Perhaps it all began because my own life had begun to feel like a tiny island of privilege adrift on a shipwrecked sea. So that after a time, being a normally conscientious person, I found it hard to go on living in my privileged serenity when other people had it so hard in the world. I didn't know what to do to help them. I started worrying.

Ordinarily I don't think worrying leads to an engagement with the world. It's more likely to become a full-time occupation that takes the place of doing anything because one can come to feel so virtuous simply by worrying.

My partner Renate and I and our friends Amy and Louise were in downtown San Francisco on the way to a trendy restaurant and we were having a good time. We were dressed up, so we must have been at the opera. In one of the doorways on our way down the street, just after we had parked the car, I spotted a bundle of rags from which the grizzled head of an old woman emerged. She was crouching there. It must have been late fall and I was wearing my new hand-woven coat from Seattle and we passed by in our high spirits and that's all there was to it. The sense of our lives going along luxuriously on their track, the sense of hers stalled in that doorway in which she was crouching. And ours going along and along, and hers stalled there, as if she and we had been set out on parallel lines that will never meet, not even in infinity. So we went on, had our dinner, did our laughing, ate well, shared a good bottle of wine. I was no longer present because I had stopped with the woman in the doorway. I was puzzling over what to do about her life, although I hadn't stopped and had done nothing. But I felt okay with myself all through dinner because, at the very least, I was worrying.

The four of us are not bad people. When we stop laughing we worry about the world and probably that night too we talked about the kind of trouble the world is in. That night, I ate half my broiled chicken, had the rest wrapped for the woman in the doorway. Then, perhaps ashamed because I hadn't ordered her an entire meal, I forgot the package on the table.

Still, worry is a form of concern. There are even times when worry suddenly shakes itself awake and begins to believe it can engage the world. This happened to me. It happened in a garden. It made me aware that gardens are themselves actively engaged in the world, if one cares to see them that way.

So there I am. I am in the garden, I am pruning the lavender. The day is drawing in, the light is fading. I feel a familiar, disturbing anguish. Usually, because this experience carries some yearning, a sense of sorrow strangely mixed up with hope and expectation, I interpret it as a longing for my dead sister, a pining after the past, an unresolved mourning. This time, abruptly, I shove these explanations away. "Admit it to yourself," I find myself saying. "Your soul is stirred because it knows there is a 'presence' in this garden. It feels it, it is aware of it, is responding to it, and that's that."

Until now I had always thought about presences, the divine, as inner experiences, psychic events. I tried to keep them psychological, to deny them "external" validity or existence beyond the confines of human personality. This time, in the garden, the distinction between inside and outside had fallen away. I felt I could call this inner yearning and knowing by its name—the soul—that I could acknowledge the existence of presences, flowing through the garden as dusk and evening came on.

Of course, I had no idea what I meant by a "presence." The word arose to indicate something ineffable, so almost there I was straining my eyes, my ears trying to catch the inaudible sound, the invisible motion. It, whatever it was, however disturbingly nameless, was coming in over the top of the redwood tree, through the branches of the flowering plum, irradiating the twilight with a cutting, luxurious coolness. There was a silence settling over the garden with a palpable weight. The sense of a message, tossed carelessly or deliberately down with the pitch of an invisible leaf. I stood there awed and rapt, recognizing the message. We are held, we are not alone in making a mess of things. Something cares about the world. A fundamental compassionate presence flows into the garden at dusk. It is here, worrying along with us.

FOR SOME OF the people I know, people on the left, many feminists, the concept of spirituality has taken on troublesome associations. To them, it suggests intolerance, fanaticism, even at times the fundamentalist capacity to murder people with whom one does not agree, during a Crusade, at an abortion clinic.

Like me, my intellectual friends associate the word "spiritual" with superstition, antireason, irrationality, a vague and sloppy mystical tendency of mind that tends to overturn all the accomplishments of the Enlightenment.

My friend Devorah objects to the word because it implies a private experience that cannot be communicated to other people. For her, spiritual folk close the door on the world. She feels left out by the spiritual, a type of elevated experience she herself has never known. From what she has observed, New Age spiritual people are always smiling, as if they have transcended the griefs and tribulations from which other, lesser people suffer.

Many of the psychoanalysts I know would translate spiritual experience as magical thinking, regressive wish-states, dissociated and psychotic conditions, none of which one would be proud to have. I have a liberal friend who cannot hear the word "spiritual" without thinking of feudalism, the submission of the individual to a hierarchy of feudal lords, priests, or their contemporary equivalent, our New Age gurus and spiritual masters. He objects to the very idea of mixing up politics with religion, as if the word "spiritual" could not possibly mean an intimately radical experience that challenges all systematic formulations, including established religions.

My friend Cathy reminds me how often churches have inspired political movements. She thinks I make too big a deal out of the opposition between the spiritual and the political, taking a division characteristic of my own background as if it were an historical norm. We argue about this over iced mint tea on a hot day. When prompted, I can see the political importance of church-inspired social movements. But I have trouble associating the intensely subjective experience of spirituality with established religion. Cathy trumps me with the civil rights movement of the sixties, church inspired, political, and yes, deeply spiritual.

With all this, why bother with the word? Pressed a bit, it evokes séances, mediums, modish Hollywood channelers—it even leads some people I know to evoke the horrors committed against children in satanic rituals. So why not abandon it? And what then? I'd feel compelled to write a book explaining some word I'd invented to describe the transformative experience with which many people are familiar. It is probably more economical to give the old word a quick spin through the heavy wash cycle, to draw it up again dripping and pure, freed from associations. When a word falls into disrepute, can't be used because of the embarrassment it causes, can't be discarded because of the use it still serves, it must be time to have a go at it again.

For the time being then, "spiritual" means for me sensitivity to an unseen order. It means, further, the capacity to take seriously one's relations to this unseen order, so that one can be transformed by it. In using the word "spiritual," I radically disown its lineage, all guilts by association, to take up the possibility that we live in a universe built fundamentally upon spiritual values, upon compassion.

This is not a fashionable idea. I myself would probably feel more comfortable if it had not taken hold of me. Over the last months I have tried on several occasions to shake it loose, only to find it growing in deeper. Therefore, I have been forced to take up the word as a legitimate subject, stripping it bare to the degree that I can, building it up again with new associations.

Spiritual experience takes place on a slippery ground between the subtle and the ineffable. The spiritual, in many of its more modest incursions, is the sort of experience you can easily brush off. It passes, often quickly. It leaves something behind that often remains hidden. There's no good reason for such slender stuff to change one, but it often does.

I am restless now that I have had my turnabout in the garden. I can't wait to find out where I'm going. My experience has left me with a sense that I will soon figure out some way to be active in the world, even if meanwhile I'm back at my desk trying to sort things out.

Although, now that I think about it, I have recently been of use to people in a way that probably reflects these changes I call spiritual.

A woman who was dying called me to sit at her bedside. For now I can say, I helped her die peacefully. I, who have always been angry at death. Death took my sister from me when I was four and a half years old. She was sixteen then. I've always been squeamish about people dying or even falling ill. My sister was dying in the small room we shared in the Bronx. No one told me that what was happening to her was dying. I went though the whole terrible business not knowing what was going on, except that she started to smell bad. Then she was gone. An old story, I've written about it before. Why do I mention it here? Left to myself, as I had been before that day in the garden, I wouldn't have been able to help a woman who was dying. She would have known it, she wouldn't have asked for me to be there day after day, as this woman did. She was not a close friend of mine, she was someone I'd known only for a few months before she started dying. But when we met, she knew and I knew we were going to do a piece of work together.

I don't know if my work with the dying woman counts

as an engagement with the world. I'd like to think so, because then I could point to one useful, tangible outcome of these changes in me. My mother always referred to meditation and other spiritual preoccupations in phrases such as this: "You won't find me or anyone I know sitting around concentrating on my navel." Another version of this could be heard on occasion: "People are starving, and what does he do? He sits there brooding about his belly button." I don't know where she picked up this knowledge of spiritual practice. Probably, in her bohemian circles in New York before she became a communist during the early thirties, there were already vegetarians and people who wore sandals in winter and made their own yogurt and practiced meditation. Perhaps indeed these people focused their attention meditatively on their navels, so as to clear the mind of other preoccupations and bring it to silence and direct it toward god. No doubt my mother, an active, world-changing sort of person, always had contempt for them. Back then, most people with a political mission were on the other side of a great divide that had split open between them and the spiritual people, so that a person of the old left, a man like my father, would have to keep his spiritual sensibility hidden—leaving to the next generation the task of bringing these far-flung dispositions back together.

To accomplish this task I am going to tell three stories. The fine thread that spins them together reminds me at times of the mysterious guide whose elusive presence keeps you going, while the whole point of the journey is to lose a sense of direction. In my first story, I shall talk about my family. Who knows? I might discover that in every sincere political commitment there is a hidden spiritual core. My second story is about my work with the dying woman. Buttressed by a family past and a mysterious piece of work in the present, I can then tell my third story, a string of adventures that has led to this writing, in which I am going to suggest that spiritual help may be necessary if we are going to engage the world ethically and politically, in the hope of repairing or even saving it.

One

MY FATHER AND I

*O*nce a year, during my childhood, my parents disagreed with each other. The discussion concerned me and could not be avoided. We all knew we had said and done the same things a year ago and would repeat them the following year but each time they engaged us.

"So," my father would say as we were finishing dinner, "I think tonight might be the night."

My mother would look at him with exasperation. "Paul," she would response, "Paul, Paul," as if she had come to believe she would never be dragged through this ordeal again.

I always took my father's side. "Well, why not? What's wrong with it? He likes it and I like it so what does it have to do with you?"

"You see?" my mother said to him. "You see?" as if his plan were to blame for his daughter's rudeness.

"I don't want you to be disappointed," he continued, along his own line of thought. "It might be tomorrow or even the day after. But I wouldn't be surprised if tonight were the night."

"I don't know, I don't know," my mother said under her breath. "Does it make sense? Paul, I ask you," she said in a louder voice, "waking a child up in the middle of the night to look at a flower?"

"I'm not a child. I'm ten years old. I wake up anyway in the middle of the night. Why shouldn't he wake me?"

"You see? Paul?"

My father considered my mother's point of view, stroked his mustache, looked at her affectionately. He took her hand. "This is what we will do," he said after a time. "I will go to her door and I will speak her name very softly. If she doesn't wake up, okay, so she doesn't and no harm will be done.

"In the middle of the night," my mother protested as my father and I gathered up the dinner dishes. He put on an apron, I tied a dish towel around my waist, my mother went off to answer the telephone. We heard her say, angrily, before she picked up the phone, "Waking a child in the middle of the night to look at a flower? Is there, I ask you, another man in the world who would carry on like this?"

"She's worried you'll be tired in the morning," he said when I shook my head about her. "She's afraid you'll be worn out for school."

"She doesn't worry when the phone rings in the middle of the night and she wakes me up with her loud voice. She just doesn't want you to wake me up because of a *flower*. That's what she doesn't want. Any other reason to wake me up is just fine with her."

"You are old enough now to see it from her point of view. To a mother it would not make much sense to wake a child up because of a flower."

"Dad! I'm not a child," I would say as the years passed. "I'm ten years old." I'm eleven years old. I'm twelve years old.

"Just think," he mused, as he hung the apron from its hook in the back porch, "by the time you are eighteen and go off to college, you will have seen it flower how many times? But tonight," he went on, as if he did not look forward to those years when I would be away, "we will have a full moon. I won't even have to bring a flashlight."

My father's cactus flowered once a year, at night. By morning, the flower would still be there but limp and sagging and no longer splendid. I remember my father coming to stand by my door to wake me up. I can still hear my mother's voice from their bedroom, reminding me to put on my shoes. I even remember the slam of the screen door as we went out into the garden. To this day, I know exactly what a night-blooming cereus looks like, a magnificent heavy-headed white flower with densely packed whorled petals. I know that I stood next to my father and gazed at the flower every year in the late summer. I have sometimes told this story as if I remembered being out there, next to him, on the wet grass in my bare feet. But I have no real memory beyond the banging shut of the door. All sensual recollection stops there, the rest is reconstruction. Even when my father managed to get me into the garden, the garden remained secret, forbidden. If I was disloyal to my mother because I wanted to see the mysterious flower, the least I could do was not remember.

Let me repeat: My mother was a woman of the old left, a communist organizer, a radical activist. What mattered to her, what created her sense of value, had been drawn from her life experience. She cared about immigrants, about the poor, about exploited, oppressed, and hungry people, all of which she herself was or had been. Her concern about the fortunes of these people was an unresting

goad to her. It kept her awake at night, organizing demonstrations, planning rallies, writing leaflets, dreaming up
legal strategies, fighting legal battles, answering emergency telephone calls. That was my mother.

My father, on the other hand, this man of the old left,
was a quiet, thoughtful, intellectual person. He loved to
play chess and played very well. On Saturdays in the late
forties and early fifties, when left-wing newspapers were
hard to peddle, he and I would go from door to door in
our neighborhood trying to sell copies of the communist
newspaper, the *People's World*. We never had much luck,
but we set out on our rounds every weekend, door to
door, although some people, once they recognized us,
hurried inside and set their dogs to barking.

I have the impression my mother felt some contempt
for this activity of my father's, since it certainly did not
accomplish much from the point of view of radical
change. It had more in common with activities of my
Berkeley neighbor who builds birdhouses for endangered
species. My mother would have regarded activity of this
sort as sentimental in the very worst sense, an indulgence
of private sensibility at collective expense, if one considers
that time spent knocking together bird habitats (or

knocking on doors) is time taken from other, more urgent social endeavors. The unemployed, the battered, the evicted, the victims of racism, the wrongfully jailed would have seemed to my mother more worthy of one's committed effort than birds. And put that way, as an absolute choice between urgencies, I suppose most people would agree with my mother. Nevertheless, I don't think she was right, although for most of my life I did think so, and this, I imagine, is one of the reasons I have always found it difficult to engage myself with the world.

As a girl my sympathies, although not my sense of what really mattered, were with my father. I thought there was something a bit sad, maybe even a little silly about his weekly rounds, but I went with him because it was better than staying home alone. My father walked with a sense of courtesy for a child, slowly, with short steps, willing to stop to look at things most adults would have counted foolish.

My father took on his paper-selling job because (I imagine) he did not regard his time spent teaching Marxism to other Marxists as having sufficient scope. He also taught Marxism to me. As I understood it then, Marxism meant there was a pattern to history and that we, as Marxists, were a knowing, dedicated part of that pattern. We were going to bring about a more just society, in which people would not have to worry about losing their jobs or living through depressions. My father explained that there would be obstacles to this achievement. Class struggle, which drove history forward, also delayed the egalitarian, socialist order for which we worked. Bosses, capitalists, landlords, factory owners, acting in the interests of their own class, would try to stop workers and farmers from achieving the conditions required to make their lives tolerable. Therefore, sooner or later revolution would come about. My mother said she would not live to see the revolution. She promised it would take place during my lifetime.

My father was a shy man. It required discipline for him to set out into our neighborhood to encounter hostile neighbors, to raise with them some of the urgent social issues of the day. He was also nobody's fool. He didn't expect to change the class consciousness of our lower middle-class neighborhood. He seemed satisfied if his reception in the neighborhood was, over time, somewhat less cool. We were a mixed community by then, a few years after we had moved into the neighborhood where my father's family had also lived. Some of our neighbors were African Americans; there were also a few Asian people, but the white folk who had not yet moved away were the most hostile to the gray-haired man in his corduroy jacket walking hand in hand with his daughter on Saturdays. I early learned not to expect much from them, although my father had clearly not yet given up. "You never know," he used to say, with his gentle humor, "the mind of man is an inscrutable document."

There was my father getting himself to do something difficult because he felt there was some small chance he might encounter or awaken a sensibility such as his own must have been before he read his first Marxist paper as a young man. He himself never said this; he never said a word about his own motivation, or that it was hard to go out selling papers door to door, but I knew it was hard, or at least I know now. Nevertheless, this activity suited him because he was a quiet-spoken person who could never have appeared on a soap box to address multitudes. Undoubtedly he would have liked to stay home on Saturdays reading a book, playing chess, pottering in the garden, but he went out to discuss politics with our neighbors.

"Good afternoon, neighbor," he would say in his old-fashioned way. "Can I interest you in a few words of conversation?" Sometimes, I had the impression that he had been practicing the phrase under his breath, to free it from all trace of his shyness. If so, he was a success. I never had to feel embarrassed for him. On other occasions, I would hear him say, in this thoughtful, quiet voice, "Allow me to introduce myself and my daughter. We live in the neighborhood and have come out this afternoon to see if we can interest you in a discussion about the world."

These conversational skills, although they were not particularly admired in my family, where my mother and I liked to shout, were in fact considerable, for they consisted of the capacity never ("never" is the accurate word) to get angry during an argument, never to respond irrationally to hostility, but always to counter it with reasoned discourse. In this respect, I cannot trace my temperamental lineage from my father because I am hot-headed and easily provoked. But his weekly walks out among our neighbors, in the hope of lighting a spark here, a slow fire of reflection there, used to seem somewhat sad to me and perhaps a bit silly.

Now they make more sense. It would have been impossible to set out every weekend into a hostile world to perform a task for which one could not expect much reward, unless one felt oneself to be in the service of something larger than the self, to which one's whole life, in its smallest and largest acts, was dedicated.

NOT THAT MY father was a spiritual man. He regarded himself, with precise pride, as an atheist, a materialist, a man liberated from religions and other superstitions. He was a scientist, a structural engineer by profession, and he loved to garden. The transformative powers of the "unseen order" by which I am fascinated would have been construed by my father in materialist terms. He was concerned about who owned the means of production, how products were alienated from the workers who produced them, how profits were made at the expense of the laboring poor. For him, it was the tensions and injustices of these social arrangements that would lead to the egalitarian socialist goal. Then, the state would wither away as no longer necessary for the regulation of human affairs. The gray-haired man and his little daughter out walking through their neighborhood on a Saturday afternoon walked with historic inevitability on their side.

My father has been dead for twenty-seven years. He died when I was twenty-seven years old. I have now lived half of my life without my father. Today, early this morning, I went rummaging in a drawer and came by chance upon his watch. I wound it, it started up and has since been keeping perfect time. In our family we were always proud of this watch, a real gold watch, inscribed to Paul Kusnitz, my father, from his employer.

Years after my father died there was a fire in which many keepsakes were lost. We lost the oil painting of my sister in her Komsomol scarf. My dad's ivory chess set was lost, and the fur pillowcase with a hammer and sickle. What has survived is so meager, each remaining object has been forced to carry the whole history of our relationship. For me, that watch has become an emblem of my father's silent influence, all its forces held in check, ready to go, long neglected until the daughter opens a drawer and finds the watch in perfect working order.

Some forty odd years later, now wearing my father's watch, I realize that what impressed me about those walks in our neighborhood was my father's sense of mission, his dedication to something unseen (the inevitability of history) that kept him going through even the hardest times.

His optimism impresses me, although back then it often irritated my mother because she had the bleaker, more embattled view of the world. She expected things to turn out badly unless you struggled tirelessly for the good. My mother and I were, I suppose, on the wrathful, world-shaking, political-agitating side of Marx. History might be drawing toward an inevitable goal, but the obstacles that rose in its path caught our attention. Both of us, mother and daughter, were here on earth to fight. We couldn't really understand my father, a more patient man. He taught me that socialism already existed in history's core, as if it were folded into the eternal necessities of things. He was a man of faith, devout, serene, certain of our human future. Although by temperament I couldn't share his optimism, I held his hand as we walked along, indescribably comforted by his certainty.

The man had a strange kind of offhand, easygoing cheerfulness, which nothing in our circumstance could explain. He had been blacklisted during the early fifties and could no longer get engineering jobs that would have made use of his skills or paid him a salary appropriate to his experience and ability. He had lost his eldest daughter some five, six years before he lost his job. He could have been bitter, weary, beaten down, indifferent. He was cheerful. This cheerfulness, strangely compatible with having been knocked around a bit and then taking a good hard look at life, is the sentiment I too have begun to entertain since I have allowed myself to consider that our chaotic, troubled, tragic human life may (nevertheless) be held by an urgent compassion.

Marx and the coming of socialism did not make my mother cheerful. She slept with her hands curled into fists beside her on the pillow. It was my job to wake her in the morning when she had been out late at a meeting. Before I left for school I would bring her the daily newspaper, sit down next to her on the bed, and say, first softly, then a bit louder: "Time to wake up, Mama." She would start awake with a look of alarm, sit straight up in bed, stare at me for a moment without recognition, tough, hard, ready to fight, grimly determined.

Was my father cheerful because he sensed a basic goodness in the human heart, which reflected a basic goodness, perhaps even ultimately a compassion, in the logic of history? If that is the impression he made on me, memory is probably tampering with the family history. When I claim that my father dressed up a hidden spiritual nature in

Marxist terms, I am rewriting his character to account for the mystical leanings in mine.

He would have objected strenuously to this idea, with good cause. Born in the first year of the twentieth century, in a small Jewish town in Russia, he was brought to America as a young boy, child of an Orthodox Jewish family. His impression of religion, spirituality, man's relationship to god was taken from Jewish life at the turn of the century among Jews who had never been assimilated into European society. For him, the religion of the *shtetl*, the reading and reciting of ancient texts in a dead language, the reliance on a god who was said to mean well by his people, yet did nothing to help them in their exile and poverty, was, from his youngest intellectual days, simply appalling. Later on, as a young man growing up in a small town in Connecticut, studying history in high school, working in his family's butcher shop, socialism appealed to him because it spoke to the immediate conditions of life here on earth, offering to rebuild a world by the principles of justice and equality.

My father, a man without bitterness, had stern things to say about man's relationship to god. He often spoke to me, his ten-year-old daughter, when we were out on those walks, about Feuerbach, the left-Hegelian philosophy he had read when he was a young man. He shared Feuerbach's view that it was man who had created god in his own image, thereby attributing to god qualities, capacities, gifts of heart and mind that were man's own attributes. "Can you imagine," my father used to say, "giving away to god everything that is worthwhile in a human being?"

I too liked the idea that we humans are capable of changing our lives, building up new social orders, expanding our scientific knowledge of the world. My father was always reading, thick books with hard covers, scientific magazines, most of the journals published on the left, the works of Marx and Durkheim. During his lunch break he would stroll over to MacArthur Park, eat his cream cheese sandwich and three dates while walking around the lake, then spend the rest of his free time in the library. He never told us this and I don't know if my mother knew. I know because school got out early one day, I had lost my house key, I had to go down to my father's office to fetch his key from him. It was lunchtime; he wasn't in the office. The other men were at their desks eating and joking together. Still, they knew exactly where he was, and sure enough I found him there, with his sleeves rolled up, tie loosened, jacket hung on the back of his chair. The library was mostly empty, so I spotted him easily in that intense, palpable quiet he had, which made you think he was in a deep communion with those historic forces from which he expected so much for the future of man.

We have had rabbis in our family, on my father's side. Some relatives say we are descended through my father's father's side from the Vilna Gaon, the great eighteenth-century Enlightenment scholar. He was well known as the enemy of Hasidism, in that time a warm-hearted, mystical sect that believed in the possibility of man's direct relationship to the divine. But according to my father's younger, only living brother, we had Hasidic rabbis in the family too, on my father's mother's side, where there was also said to be the gift for healing through the laying on of hands (a detail worth noting: it will become important in my next story).

My father never said that religion was the opiate of the people, but he shook his head when we passed a church or the temple on Adams Boulevard, with one of those quiet sighs he had. We always stopped at the Jewish bakery for rye bread with sissel; dry, twisted, sugar-dusted cookies called kichel; an onion roll for me to munch as we walked. We were on our way back now with our stack of papers and it was usually the same stack with which we had started out, rarely if ever diminished. Our work was done for the day, we wouldn't be knocking at any more doors, my father was relieved, although he would never have said so. He held my hand and whistled. I don't think I was a particularly observant child, but I managed to notice that this whistling never occurred when we set out on our walks. It came after the knocking and the trudging on, the synagogue and the head shake, the bread and the onion roll.

WHEN I WAS a small girl, about three years old, I developed a theory about the sun and moon. I told my mother that the moon was always there in the sky but we could not see it because during the daytime the sun was brighter. This counted as a sign of precocity in my family but I do not think I was talking so much about sun and moon as about my mother and father, and the way the dramatic scale of her activity blinded one to him, drowned him out in her greater brilliance.

My father would have agreed with my mother that value is established by the relationship an act holds to the transformation of the social order. He would not have thought of his paper-selling as likely to do much in that regard. He (I repeat) would have dismissed my idea that his relationship with the world was spiritual.

Nevertheless, my father's acts had mysterious consequences. I observed these as a child, because they affected me and made a difference in my life. When mysterious consequences flow from small acts, it is easy to get the impression our lives are bound together, held in a web of intention and compassion. This is another spiritual idea my father would not have endorsed.

About the time my father and I were selling newspapers on Saturdays, a cross was burned on the lawn of the first African American family who came to live in our neighborhood. My mother organized a vigil to welcome our new neighbors, to let them know there were decent people among us who would not allow them to be driven out. After that, other African American families moved in, then Japanese Americans moved in, and soon the white folk were in a minority. The neighborhood became a fascinating place for a child, especially the Baptist church on our boulevard, where the singing drew me to the front door.

I remember well the way my mother charged out to gather the decent people in our neighborhood for the neighborhood vigil. Until recently, I didn't think much about my father's role in this. (Of course my father and I were in the vigil, too, but we didn't organize it.) After the cross-burning, when the neighborhood was still largely white, another dark-skinned man moved in a few blocks away and was now tolerated (but also isolated) by his neighbors.

It was with this man my father struck up a conversational friendship on Saturdays. They were both quiet-spoken men, I could see that it was a relief to both of them to have found each other, which was a relief to me, too, because I used to fear that my father's feelings would be hurt by our neighbors' rebuffs. I played with the man's dog while the two men talked. This man began to buy our newspaper regularly, so now there was always his house to look forward to, where we knew we had one reliable sale. He was a janitor in the local school system and used to walk home from work just after dark, which may have accounted for the fact that in passing our house he noticed a car parked across the street first one night, then the next, and the next, which made him suspicious, so he knocked at our door for the first time to tell my parents. That is how we came to know my mother was being followed by the FBI. Because we knew this we were silently able to start preparing for her arrest, although when it came, a few weeks later, we were taken by surprise. Still, I imagine that I, an eleven-year-old girl, was somewhat less terrified than I might have been thanks to this neighbor, who knew what was at stake, who took a risk, who looked scared, who let us know what he thought was happening.

There may be a place where socialist humanism and spiritual politics meet, parallel lines finally twisted together by infinity. My gray-haired father and the dark-skinned stranger who had become his neighbor could be thought of as emblems of brotherly love. Or, I could cast them as I would have some years ago, thinking back on those childhood days, as a living exemplar of the socialist man history would one day produce in abundance.

My father's bond to this man was in some sense a spiritual bond, because it was based on an immediate kinship with a stranger, a man from a different race whom my father immediately recognized. Our neighbor's behavior when we were in danger also seems spiritual to me: it took courage, caring, involved a risk on behalf of people he hardly knew. Taken together, this spiritual affinity between the men might be understood as part of the mysterious consequence generated from small acts of engagement with the world. For a chain of consequence was set in motion by my father's pleasure at finding a neighbor friendly to his radical thought. It is this sort of consequence we tend to overlook when we think about the world through the eyes of someone like my mother, with her vision of the politics of total commitment on a grand scale, as if our small acts were not part of larger currents, social and spiritual, by which even our daily lives are perhaps regularly informed.

Did I, unknown to myself as a young girl, already experience my father as a spiritual person? Did he make this impression on me because of my own dormant tendency to experience the world in spiritual terms, however absent these were from the family conversation? Or were my parents unknowingly in touch with the (forbidden, disowned) religious core of Marxism? Their need to serve, to live out their lives according to a larger purpose, their lifelong preoccupation with the lot of the poor, their sense of historic mission—these they held in common with each other, this the source of their enduring kinship, these the common passions I find folded into the radical structure of the spiritual people I have met.

Our social gatherings on the left, even our most blatantly political rallies and demonstrations, always held a religious character. In them, I felt us thaw away into an ecstatic union with the others, which my mother described as entering the collective, my father as a foretaste of the socialist world.

A WORD MORE about mysterious consequences.

Our neighbor, the dark-skinned janitor, had a niece who lived some blocks away in our neighborhood. She used to visit him on occasional weekends. After a time she and I began to play together with the brown dog while the two men talked. This niece later happened to go to my junior high school. We didn't become friends, although we said hello to each other when we passed in the hall or on the playground. Nevertheless, after my mother was arrested for attempting to overthrow the government by force and violence, in that first difficult time when other kids stopped talking to me, this girl occasionally walked home with me, as if she were just stopping in to say hello to her uncle, who lived a few streets away.

Thinking back on these walks, which meant a lot to me, I am inclined to see them as belonging with the consequences that grew out of my father's satisfaction in having found a neighbor who was interested in ideas. This man told my father he had never thought some of the thoughts he read in our left-wing newspaper and that he was happy to have come across them. That too was a consequence of my father's Saturday walks, which led to the man's friendship to us in a hard time, which led to his niece walking home from school with me.

My father used to say, when we were out on those walks, things I never heard him say at home. Perhaps they were his spontaneous thoughts, not mediated by his stern sense of ideological probity. He would say, "You never know, do you, what makes a difference. The life of man," he would sigh, "what a fathomless enigma." "Daddy, why do you talk to yourself?" I used to ask him. "Well," he would say, "I have always liked to converse with a man who has an intelligent daughter." Then he would shake his head, as if to dismiss these enigmatic thoughts, which were leading in a direction he would have preferred his thoughts not go.

He once quoted, with much hesitation, a man he deliberately did not name. I have remembered the words of this (then, to me) unknown thinker for more than forty years. "Socialism is not a science, a sociology in miniature: it is a cry of pain . . ."

This is Emile Durkheim, the founder of modern sociology, whom most communists of my father's generation would not have been reading, probably because Durkheim thought of Marxism as merely *one* possible way of studying society.

Socialism as a cry of pain. My father's need to say this must have been very strong, or he would never have repeated to me Durkheim's conviction that socialism was not a science. My father had probably read Durkheim as a young man, before his own Marxist identity had solidified, then rarely mentioned him, perhaps only that once, out walking with his daughter. Socialism as a cry of pain. The followers of Marx (as I knew them in my childhood) on fire with moral passion. The world-historical mission to which one's life was pledged. Marx's intransigent vision of the withering away of classes and the state. That apocalypse has nothing in common with the Enlightenment tendency of historical thought in the nineteenth century. These passions and visions are spiritual.

No one in my family knew or could possibly have imagined that the appeal of Marx was, for us, a profoundly religious business. That thesis has been left to me. Yet I have never felt closer to my parents than I do now in my paradoxical, illegitimate, subversive spiritual reading, spun out against their scientific and materialist values.

My father lost his job during the early fifties. He was indifferent to the loss of prestige, although he had been working for a large company where he had been highly valued and much promoted, until the company began to take on government projects. He suffered from losing his job; he did not know if he could find another. He suffered so much he had to spend three days in bed, with a mysterious, unnamed illness I would now call anxiety. In those bleak days between jobs he was not cheerful, he was silent, we did not go out for our Saturday walks. Eventually, he was persuaded to start a business of his own with a fellow engineer, also a Marxist. Almost immediately, he disliked being in business.

"Business," I heard him say to my mother, "is not suitable for a socialist man."

"Socialist men in capitalist societies have to earn a living. Is it better when the profits go to the boss?"

"It is a question," my father said sadly, "of what one has to do to earn the profits. Could I live with myself, could I fall asleep at night, if I made my profits exploiting another man's labor?"

A few weeks later my father gave up his business and began to look for work. I remember those evenings when he came in tired and discouraged, helped me set the table, put the potatoes up to cook. "Hey, Dad, no luck?" I'd ask casually, because I knew he didn't want me to worry. "Don't worry," he answered, "I will find work. A man of my experience," he would say with a suppressed sigh, "will find a way to be useful. Sooner or later," he went on, with no bitterness that I could detect, "someone will realize they can profit from my knowledge."

He was right. Many months later, my father was hired by a man who told him that he knew my mother was on trial for being a communist. "He is a good man," my father said, when he told us about his new job, "an honorable man. There are people like that everywhere, also in business."

For the rest of his life, my father's salary was not what it might have been. This irritated my mother but I know for a fact that my father never minded. His job was secure.

If my father had gone into business for himself, he

would have had to work on weekends. An ambitious man would have accepted this as inevitable. My father, the Marxist, loved to garden. When we were not out selling papers on the weekend, he was turning over the soil near the fence, where there was a lot of gravel. Eventually, we grew our own corn, potatoes, green onions, beets, radishes, cucumbers, and sorrel, which we ate as a cold soup all summer long. He cultivated roses, lilies, dahlias, birds of paradise, carnations, hibiscus, and camellias. We never went to visit a friend, a comrade, a member of our family without a bundle of flowers tied with a string and wrapped in wet newspaper. Members of the family also received large bundles of sorrel because sorrel in those days never appeared in the market. My mother disliked the wet bundles my father prepared because they left damp spots on my dress. But when we arrived at our destination, I a bit damp, the bundles still dripping, the newspaper soggy, we all took pride in the luxuriant roses, the perfect camellias, the sturdy stalks of paradise all carefully chosen to be the best the garden had to offer.

My childhood story has an interesting twist, which once again involves my mother. The thoughtful man who was our neighbor, who had begun to buy the *People's*

World from us, eventually moved back to the South because his mother was ill. But his niece and I had grown fond of each other and she came to visit us a lot, so that my mother, when she got out of jail, got to know her well. In the summers we used to dance together in our backyard with three or four drummers from our school, and that girl was a wonderful dancer. Soon, my father talked to her mother, who worked hard and didn't have money to spare, and when that girl was starting to get into trouble (skipping school, shoplifting, cutting graffiti into the back seats of the bus), so that she might have been kicked out of school, or worse, my mother arranged for her to get a scholarship to a dance school run by one of our family's left-wing friends. And so it came about that this girl became a professional dancer and was one of the very few kids I know from that neighborhood who left it for the larger world. Or so I thought. Some years ago I found out that she had left alright, and had come back, fairly well known, and had been teaching dance out of a garage a few blocks away, near the grammar school and the Jewish bakery. I don't think it is far-fetched to see some link between this return of my childhood friend to our neighborhood and those walks my father used to take, the newspapers he was selling, the conversations he had with her uncle who was a thoughtful man and must have encouraged her to walk home from school with me, where she met my mother. I like to imagine that just one of her dance students in the converted garage was saved from something difficult that might have happened to her if she had not met this teacher, just as who knows what might have happened to me if this teacher, when she was a girl, had not walked home with me from school in that difficult time after my mother was arrested.

My mother, thinking back on her life, would surely not remember this story about my school friend who made her way back into the neighborhood where her uncle, who used to buy papers from my father, had been living when we went out on our Saturday walks. This event would not have counted for much in my mother's house. But I bet anything my father, if he were living, would remember her.

WHEN I TRY to catch my father in his most characteristic gesture I find him in the garden. There, he is involved in an extraordinary stillness. I don't think he hummed or whistled, but a lilting pleasantness inhabited the silence and filled me, even back then when I had no word for it, with awe. My father taught me to turn the earth, dig holes, loosen the roots on small potted plants, sprinkle the hole with fertilizer, press the earth down hard around them. I liked this work. It lasted for only a few weeks each spring. The rest of the year, my dog and I spent a lot of time in the garden. But I was rarely out there with my father. I preferred, it seems, to stay alone in my room (when my father was in the garden my dog would not come inside). In my room I was lonely and restless, tinkered about with my wood-burning set, couldn't get absorbed in anything, often found myself at the window looking out into the garden. Memory has gathered together these isolated moments, frozen them, fixed a meaning on them.

Today, I would say that it was the stillness, the hours of silent, reverential work in which my father was absorbed that troubled me, as if I already knew it was forbidden to know my father in this way, through this deeply concentrated, devotional side of him, which has left me lifelong with the impression that gardening is a form of prayer.

Emotions we tend to think of as spiritual come easily to

some people and must have come naturally to my father. How else could they have been transmitted to his daughter, the lonely watcher at the window, who did not dare to go outside? The capacity to worship, which I myself have, is a capacity I would claim for my father, if worship is a surge of deep emotion in response to the beauty of slowly growing things.

Reverence, too; he had that, along with a tremendous tenderness for living things. My father was devoted to the small children we met when out on our walks, the neighborhood kids who came romping into the garden whenever he was at work (I watched them from my window). He was patient with the dog we had recently brought into our household. That dog got a regular Saturday bath between the gardening and the paper-selling, and he had learned the rhythm of this bathing. When my father came in with fresh vegetables for lunch, our dog raced past him into the house, scurried under the spare bed in my bedroom. The bed was close to the floor; even I couldn't get under there to fetch my dog. We moved the bed, the dog moved along with it. We brought broom handles, the rag mop. That dog was not afraid of us. He enjoyed this game as much as my father did, although it sometimes took us a good hour or more to fetch the dog out and even then it was a battle to keep him in the soapy water in the washtub on the back porch. This bathing had to get done before my mother came home; it was not her sort of business. With its soap and its suds and its disobedient dog and its wild shaking of water all over, it would have driven her crazy.

I once saw my father approach a flower on a damaged stem. It must have been summer, the garden was full of flowers. Even a very devoted gardener could have gone for the rose with a fast clip, but not my father. There was tape and glue, twine and thread in his toolbox, the flower was (perhaps) restored by his pottering, tying, taping, tending.

How a temperament of this type came to be associated with the inevitability of violent revolution remains a mystery. My mother and I seemed born to revolution, that was the business of my mother's house. But my father? I suspect my father thought very little about revolution because he had simply moved on into the socialist future, where people would give what they had to the collective, work a few hours in the morning, fish or garden in the afternoon, write poetry in the evening. He implied, each time he said he was a socialist man, that the qualities he most valued in human beings were so incompatible with his society, one could only imagine them in a man of the future, that socialist man in whose image he lived his life.

My father's small acts of kindness and concern required some self-discipline, an urging of himself past the tendency to do the easiest thing one can do on a Saturday afternoon, but they remained nevertheless temperamentally appropriate to him, belonging as they did to his natural sphere of interest, connecting him through his own temperament to the larger currents that shape our world. We might take for granted the natural exercise of human decency until we find ourselves failing to engage in small acts of concern because the world has begun to look so troubled that small acts have begun to seem insignificant.

My father believed it would be best if all people were capable of giving their entire life to acts of social responsibility. But my father was not a man of this type. He also could not content himself with concerned acts that did not affect the larger world, although he characteristically engaged in them. Therefore, he was faced with a dilemma. What was right for him temperamentally seemed incorrect from a political point of view.

This self-division is characteristic of many of us who

have a desire to make the world a more just place, but who feel a kind of dogged futility that makes it difficult to engage in any kind of political act because most acts seem either too large or too small to us, requiring either too much from us or issuing in too little consequence. Therefore, we do nothing.

Last night I dreamed that I was lecturing about how we, the privileged in a society of growing poverty, racism, desperation, are damaged by the way we close ourselves off to knowledge of our less privileged neighbors. While I talked I was wrapping myself in stiff gauze to demonstrate how this refusal of knowledge was smothering me.

I know I was trying, even from within my dream, to awaken myself. But what was this awakening supposed to be? I will not wake up to discover I am, after all, a woman like my mother. Of course, not everyone has had a mother who was an activist on a grand scale. But such a figure, endowed with the capacity to act grandly, informs our political musing. Most people with a sense of social responsibility, who nevertheless do not act, are often (if unknowingly) measuring the acts of concern they might spontaneously enact against a social imperative that immediately dwarfs them.

When my father died, we were taken by surprise when hundreds of people showed up for the memorial service we held for him, this shy, quiet man who liked to stay home and play chess. We were even more surprised when one person after the next came forward to tell about acts of concern my father had performed, in secret, throughout his life, and which he had pledged them never to mention to anyone else, a secret they kept until he died. (For instance, I think the "scholarship" my mother arranged for my childhood friend at the dance school may have been endowed by my father and that even my mother would not have known of this.) I am quite sure my father would not have wanted people to come forward after his death to tell about these acts he may have felt were small and relatively insignificant when measured on a grand, historic scale. Or maybe he was just one of those modest people who like to remain hidden. Or maybe he thought my mother and I might have laughed at him, the way we would also have laughed at the neighbor building birdhouses for endangered species, or the woman who rescues greyhounds, or the man who is concerned about the cutting down of trees and the spotted owl.

If the small is problematic, the large has its problems

too. It tends to encourage a sense of contempt for anything that is not as large as itself, so that soon one's work
with the mentally ill, or the homeless, or the battered can
come to seem futile when set against the large numbers of
mentally ill and battered who wander the streets beyond
the reach of one's acts of concern. Their condition, it is
said, can only be changed by revolution or other forms of
radical social transformation, so that soon one is not
doing what one might because one is defeated by not
doing what one should, and the process of closing off sets
in, and before long one is wrapped in a numbing, life-
threatening indifference, as I was in my dream.

I LIKE TO think my father would have followed me in these
thoughts. Certainly, he would have agreed that we do not
know much about the consequences of our acts. Perhaps
he was also aware of how the small grows by its connection to other small things, to other acts, gestures,
moments of courage or concern. If this is so, my wandering train of thought has led finally to the reconciliation
between my mother's house and my father's garden. For it
may be that all our acts unfold by knocking into other acts
sent spinning on their way to affect yet others, in a vast

chain of consequence that may in the end lead to the transformation of the world my mother desired when she set out every morning to do big things, such as stopping deportations of people who had a right to remain in America and deserved just immigration laws.

In some abstract scheme of value, human misery may count higher than the homelessness of birds. But my neighbor, who builds birdhouses for endangered species, if she were not building birdhouses would not be down on Telegraph Avenue helping the homeless. The capacity for political activity on a large, life-consuming scale may be a gift, like perfect pitch in music, or the ability to create a masterpiece. If the desire for political activity on a large scale is a temperamental endowment, or an expression of an imperative inner need to organize, speak out, protest, fight for rights, these traits will not become the nature of all people, no matter how insistently we strike the moral note, urging them to wake up, become conscious, recognize injustice, act. Undoubtedly it is too bad that we are not all people like my mother, but the fact remains that some of us are people like my father, who never learned to resolve the contradiction with which he lived out his life.

My father, in my version of him, was a man of deep

spiritual feeling who had devoted his life to a political cause. This cause required a commitment to activism that was not temperamentally appropriate to him. In his time, in his world, the idea of a left spiritual politics would have been inconceivable.

But a good spiritual shaking up may shatter our protective indifference to the world. The sense of an unseen order, brooding attentively over our lives, restores purpose to individual acts of concern. When we can act, even in small ways, we can more easily take in a desperately troubled world, even one for which we have no comprehensive solution.

This taking in of the world is the act by which spiritual politics begin. We turn back to look, we stop long enough to see, we let the world enter. Where we were once afraid to feel concern, we are now troubled. Where we were once indifferent to what we had heard, we now listen. Where we once avoided conversation, we now bring up the topic. Then, one day, when we would otherwise have walked by the dog being kicked by its owner, the old woman crouched in the doorway, we respond. For taken together, as the total investment of the human community in acts of concern, these small acts, each appropriate to the temperament of the person acting, begin to sum up. Add together all the local, individual, specific, particular, private acts, which represent a concern for trees and dying oceans and bad air and homeless people and the mentally ill and the unemployed and the impoverished and the battered and abused wives and the damaged children, and the recently laid off and the long unemployed, and those who manage to get welfare and those who do not, and those with insurance problems and those who cannot get decent medical care, and those who die too young from violence and those who live too long to have friends left, and those who are addicted and those who are addicting others, add all this together and you find that each one of us, doing what we are able to do, doing something, involved in our small acts according to our temperamental inclination, our affinity for those less advantaged whom we reach out to help, are contributing in fact to a global effort of concern, in which it does not really matter which acts are larger or smaller or more important or more lasting or more consequential, or which should come first while others are postponed. Of course, as my mother would say, these small acts, left to themselves, do not stop wars from occurring, or halt the spread of fascism or the collapse of economic systems or the decline of great states. But who after all knows where these small acts lead? At the very least, they set in motion a considerable decency to set against the considerable violence so vividly alive in our world today.

Spiritual politics. For me, the words are charged with so much tension and antithesis it is very difficult to bind them together in a single phrase, virtually impossible to make my father their standard-bearer. My loyalty to my father seems to grow up between the words, pushing them apart, forcing them back into their oppositional camps. I think my father was a man who lived his whole life between the tension and contradiction of these two words. That alone explains the mystery of his nature, so much of it hushed, invisible, unseen, never mentioned, yet so strangely influential, like that watch keeping perfect time after twenty-seven years in a drawer.

EARLY IN THE mornings, in that particular twilight in which you cannot say whether light or dark will follow, I sometimes try to imagine my father's life stretched out, larger than he lived it. Then I play with the idea of a grand political movement that would embrace the qualities of my father's silenced self, the spiritual self we all, during my childhood, agreed not to notice.

I could offer my garden. Chess might be played between discussions; a bit of gardening might break up the afternoon; children would be free to climb the tree ladder or pack themselves onto the wooden swing. In my father's name, I imagine a dozen samovars all over the garden, plates of his favorite poppy-seed cake, people of all ages who want to acknowledge one another, who are prepared to believe in the possibility of a future, who ask, from this gathering together, the inspiration to go on, often in solitude, in their devotions to the small.

A movement of this type, as I like to imagine it, might gather its members once or twice a year to take note of the collective power that has been generated by individual acts of concern. Such a movement, by observing the totality that grows out of small acts, would no doubt begin to generate a collective identity of concern. So that sooner or later, each of us, acting as an I, would yet know herself to be part of a loosely constructed we that grows into a movement of social engagement whose actions move in consistently expanding concentric circles, from the individual and local, through the more general, to the most severe global issues of social injustice without ever losing track of its roots in the small.

This devotion to the small is the spiritual core of political acts. As a devotion, it takes note of the power of the small and observes its potential for generating consequence. That is what makes it political.

The small, it might be said, spins the threads that weave the net that catches the world. This world-net we cast, almost unwittingly, from our gathering together of individual acts, carries a particular value. When this value, of what is intimate, immediate, participatory, personally engaged, grows strong enough to be noticed by a disintegrating society, we are standing face to face with a movement for social justice that may be different from other spiritually inspired movements. This movement, built on the widest possible span of social concerns, would be highly tolerant and marked by an absence of dogma. It would have no leaders and no enemies either. Although spiritual, this movement, as I imagine it, would have no contempt for daily life, would not attempt to transcend and overcome the material world, but would endlessly and devotedly potter and tinker with it, our sacred natural habitat.

Therefore, there would be room not only for practitioners of the small, but for the meat and potato practical workers and for those people like my mother, the dedicated activists, the world-changing idealists. There would be room for those of us who like to think more, act less, but undoubtedly would be inspired to act more in a community that welcomed bit-part (en)actors. Here, in this political garden, with its samovars and children and chess and organized discussions, my mother's house and my father's garden would have found their reconciliation.

My father died long before Berkeley's gardening activists were on the scene, but I imagine that both he and my mother would have welcomed them warmly to our garden and to the political movement I have begun to imagine in their names. My father and mother both would see vast potential in the cultivation of community gardening sites. Perhaps the three of us together would attend the debates of the Berkeley Planning Commission about turning over wasted public space for community gardens. I can imagine my father, shy man though he was, getting up to argue for the gardens' potential to bring neighbors together. My mother would point out that gardens could provide food for the poor. My father would be concerned about recreational space for children. My mother would advocate the creation of childcare centers. I would speak about the way gardens create beauty in blighted urban environments.

In this fantasy the secret gardens of my father's spiritual thought would have become overtly political without losing anything of their visionary nature. Spiritual people, such as I now seem to be, people who poke around in the garden, who occasionally converse with spirits and presences, could proudly bring to this committed garden their reports from the unseen world. If there are messages of compassion currently being sent to us from unknown quarters, it might be very useful to receive and distribute them.

Two

A WOMAN IS DYING

*I*n our family death took place in whispered conversations. That meant it never took place at all. When my sister died I was told she had gone away to school. Many years later my mother told me they had hoped I would forget her. Therefore no one ever spoke of her again. Death meant silence, aversion, uneasiness, a disruption in memory, a shadowy guilt if a thought of the hushed one happened to occur. A year or two after my sister died, the phone rang during dinner. I knew with a stunned, absolute certainty before anyone picked up the telephone that my father's mother had died. A couple of years later, when Aunt Fanny, my father's eldest sister, died, the same thing happened again. The telephone call at dinner, the instantaneous recognition, as if I had been waiting all those years for the death call that would never arrive to inform the child who knew everything.

This story I am about to tell, about work I have done recently with a dying woman, would have been deeply disturbing to my mother. She would have frowned, toyed with her coffee cup, found a reason to leave the room. My father always gave me a fair hearing. His listening let a story drag itself out; when you were talking to him, you said more than you had intended, you even said things with which you knew he would not agree. Nevertheless, I would have found it difficult to tell this story to my father. It might have reminded him of his own mother, of her reputation for healing through the laying on of hands, a story that appeared occasionally in family gossip, repeated by one, scoffed at by another. He would have understood the love involved in my story, but would have been skeptical about some of its more mysterious details. He would have wondered why it was necessary to speak about things better done in silence, then forgotten.

This is a love story, a mystery, and a triangle. Until it occurred, I had been trying, unsuccessfully, to find the work that would move me out of the closed circle of my life into a larger participation in the world. I knew this work would have to be intimate, personal, full of risk. I knew it might be work I already did, if I could let myself take this work further, push its limits, undo its restraints.

If I were telling this story to my parents my mother would grow restless, my father would hear me out to the end.

Told, then, as if I were telling it to him:

Death hasn't been easy for us, I would say, and is the last thing in the world I would have imagined as my vocation.

AS I START to tell this story to my father, I enter a quick spin of vertigo. It is a bit like leaping off the present without a parachute, a few treacherous landing places, an easy glide past the steep roof of a barn, and there I am at the door to my waiting room. I am about to meet the mother of my client Marcie.

I had of course formed an impression of her over the years. A tall, slim, independent, tough, engaging woman, with a sense of humor, a quick temper, a poignant desire to make up to her daughter for a difficult childhood.

Lynn and I shake hands. She is softer than I have imagined, perhaps because she has been ill. For the last half year she has undergone chemotherapy following an operation for colon cancer. Our meeting seems simple, conversational, the casual fulfillment of a wish mother and daughter have had over many years to bring the three of us together.

Nevertheless, during our conversation my eyes meet Lynn's. The gaze holds, deepens. This happens several times; I sense an unasked question. Perhaps, in answer to it, or because of my own need to speak, I tell her about my sister's death. She watches me sympathetically while I am talking, sifting out (I think) the message I am trying to send. I too wonder: What exactly is this message?

Perhaps I have wanted to tell her I am on familiar terms with death, having known it early, then been forced to think about it for the rest of my life to free myself from its devastation. She is there, I decide, to check me out. Whatever the doctors have said, she knows her recovery may not be complete.

She asks to embrace me when she and Marcie are leaving. She isn't a hugging sort of woman, I know that already. She grips my shoulders with her hands, I put my hands on her shoulders. There we stand, taking each other's measure. If the time comes when she has something hard to ask of me, I probably will not shy away from the question.

That first meeting took place in February 1993. A year

later the cancer had spread to the bone. Lynn began radiation treatments on April 11, 1994. The next day the three of us met for the second time, once again in my office.

Marcie sits in the beige chair, where she sat during our many years of work together. Now, in the chair next to her, is Lynn, a beautiful, gaunt woman of fifty-eight, with strong features sharpened by suffering. Marcie is wearing glasses. Her composed, youthful face (this face that has grown so dear to me over the years) today is not giving away secrets. Her glasses reflect me when she turns to face me. If she is scared, torn up, heartbroken, her face will not let her mother know.

From the moment we sit down together, Marcie adjusting the pillows because her mother is in pain, I know the older woman has come to ask something of me, this time directly.

There is conversation about wills, lawyers, what will be left to whom, whether there is any hope left. Marcie is grave, affectionate, older than she was a few months ago, when we ended the formal period of our work together. I am caught up in what is being said, but at the same time observing us from a distance. The two women are impressive. Their mutual honesty, their way of saying what they have to say, not mincing words. Marcie's mother says, "I don't think I will live out the year."

Marcie says, with that tough humor she and her mother share, "Sometimes I think my mother is willing to die because it is the only way to retire from her business."

Marcie can cry without crying. I have noticed this many times before. Now, as she leans toward her mother to adjust the pillows, the daughter's face shows a fugitive grief, tenderness, anxious concern, patience. Then, a will to fight, to keep her mother alive as long as possible, to see her through when that becomes necessary. I notice the way Marcie leans toward Lynn, protectively, then shifts back toward me, almost imperceptibly. Then, Lynn tells me a story about her father. Marcie has not heard the story before, although she had been with her grandfather at home when he died of cancer. In a period when his pain became almost unbearable, he had screamed out asking Marcie's mother to help him die, begging her to shoot him, pleading with her. Lynn says, "I've never been able to forget that screaming. I hadn't forgotten. But I couldn't help him."

Again, that look, taking my measure.

The unasked question is coming closer.

Lynn's gaze is an anguished shout heard from a distance, setting all your resources on edge. You want to run. Toward? Away? To help? To abandon? To save your own skin? To give something desperately vital to another person? And what if you don't have it? What if, with the best will in the world, you are not able to help?

After a time, Marcie says, very carefully, "My mother had me promise I would never let that happen to her."

Some questions don't get asked. If you want to hear them you have to respond as if they've been asked. If you miss the opportunity, the silent questions will die away, you will have answered in the negative, no word will have been spoken.

I'm relieved when I hear myself say, "Well, if that is the agreement you've reached, and you need my help, of course I will give it."

"You understand what I am asking?" Lynn has not taken her eyes off my face.

"If the pain becomes too great, you want me to help Marcie to help you die."

I have always known I would help anyone I loved, regardless of the consequences. I may have formed this resolution unknowingly during the long nights of my sister's dying in the room we shared. Those are the risks you take for love. Are they the risks you take for a stranger?

I probably know more about Lynn than I do most of my friends. She is only a few years older than I am. I too was a young mother, married at eighteen. I know what it is like to divorce young, have unpredictable moods, direct anger at a small child. Nothing that concerns this mother and daughter is alien to me.

Marcie has moved perceptibly in my direction.

"Do you know how to do it?"

"We'll have to find out."

When Marcie was growing up, Lynn was young, beautiful, and hardworking. She drove a convertible, had blond hair, she would gather up Marcie and her friends and carry them off to Clear Lake, Yosemite, Disneyland, Santa's Village. Marcie and her mother shared a bedroom in her grandparents' house with their dog, Susie. Marcie remembers her mother's perfume bottles, her cowlneck cashmere sweaters.

Marcie keeps her eyes on me. I know this although I am looking at her mother. I can feel the responsibility that has just settled on my shoulders. I am going to help Marcie help her mother to die if Lynn should ask me.

Because I am not equal to this task, I will have to grow into it.

Lynn says, into the enormous silence that has grown up between us, "Do you promise?"

In that moment, I know that Lynn does not have long to live.

When they are leaving, Lynn puts her arms around me. As I begin to hug her, Marcie reminds me, "You can't hug her very hard, she's in a lot of pain."

My arms grow light. Am I afraid to hug this woman who might be dying? Then, my arms are moving with an intention of their own. They are settling slowly around the dying woman's shoulders. They scarcely touch her, yet seem to have enfolded her in a palpable radiance to which she hands herself over with a resigned, crumpling gesture, as if her will has now, after a lifetime of struggle, finally collapsed. Love is what I feel for her. It is a fierce, hot protective presence. It has a wild, willful intensity. It believes in itself against all odds. Am I experiencing Marcie's extravagant love for her dying mother? I have become weighty, solid, large-breasted, reliable, tranquil. Because of this love I will be incapable of letting her down. I know this, she knows this, Marcie has always known it. But what

I have just become I have never been before. If Marcie has trusted me to be capable of this, her trust has made it possible.

HERE, RIGHT AT the beginning, something has happened because of love. If I were talking to my father I would now grow uneasy. I would not like to tell him about that episode when my arms set out on a mission of their own. By the time they embraced the dying woman she was no longer a stranger. I loved her. To set this love apart from the knotted, deeply rooted, far more complex love that grows up between people who share a history, I call this a spiritual love.

My father would have taken this love for granted. He would have seen no reason to call it spiritual. He certainly would not have come up with the psychoanalytic explanation of countertransference, by which so much genuine love between people who work intimately together is made recognizable, simply as love.

Undoubtedly, I loved Marcie's mother through Marcie. I was influenced in this love by the years of work Marcie and I had done together. I brought to this moment at the door a wish to help a dying person, as I had not been able to help my sister during childhood. I too have a mother who is infirm, who is now, at the age of ninety-three, always almost dying. There, at the door, as we were saying good-bye, I was, yes, doubly a daughter prepared to love a dying mother.

Past and present circumstance, the long relationship I already had with the daughter, would be sufficient to account for the love I felt. Even the way my arms took on a radiance, so that they could hug without hugging, embrace without pressure, even that could be explained by the heightened, troubled drama of the moment.

The spiritual element in this passing moment, which instantaneously made me different from the person I had been the moment before, was my understanding that I would receive the help I needed in order to give help to the dying woman. I was not alone; I would know what I needed to know when the time came; dying, death itself would hold no fear for me.

Because we three shared this experience a bond was created between us that made us all larger than ourselves. Divine love, they say, draws those whom it seizes beyond themselves. If anyone of us had been even slightly less receptive than we were as we stood at the door, this opening into the spiritual dimension might not have taken place.

Stories have a mind of their own. Some tend to muse, meander, circle back, start over again. Others tend to throw up roadblocks. This refusal to get going, this stubbornness, usually has a purpose. The writer is meant to brood, grow frustrated, try to get on with it, be yanked back. This story with so many beginnings—how stubbornly it returns to that moment at the door, the threshold that must be approached from different paths before one can pass through into the story.

If my father were listening he would have begun to smile. To know my father was smiling you would have to read a slight deepening of the wrinkles around his eyes, an imperceptible reddening of his nose, the quickly passing, almost tender expression of knowing sympathy for the storyteller, out on a limb, trying to get back on course, scared of where the story is going, probably embarrassed.

That moment at the door, that roadblock, that threshold? When we get beyond it, this story will take off on a mysterious path, on which birth and death, for a brief time, will be made companions. It will be Marcie who will bring them together, unexpectedly, after years of struggle to become a mother.

This is the story that must be told before we can cross the threshold.

SINCE CHILDHOOD MARCIE has experienced profound insecurity. In time, over years of work together, we have come to believe this sensitivity has much to do with her parents' divorce when she was a year old, her mother's unpredictable moods, an uprush of anger followed by an inscrutable emotional barrier.

When Marcie was four years old she and her mother went back to live with her mother's parents. Grandfather and mother ran a tire business from their backyard. When the business began to take off, they acquired a property and moved into it. Marcie was left in the care of her grandmother, who had had a severe menopausal breakdown, complicated by alcoholic problems. She was paranoid. At times, she locked the doors and blockaded them with chairs. Grandmother had episodes of drinking, smoking, sitting in her chair, talking out loud to herself, laughing, singing, ignoring her granddaughter.

These facts have caused me to wonder why mother left

Marcie alone with the old woman. Marcie has explained her mother's state of mind. She had been eighteen years old when her daughter was born. She was a single mother raising an only child. She had felt a failure at marriage. The relationship with her father, and the work bond with him, meant a lot to her. At times, she was a tough, disciplined woman who often seemed under pressure and worked too hard.

Marcie grows up wanting to build the family life she never had as a child, but when things go wrong she tends to think the trouble was meant to happen. She asks: Is there something wrong with me? Am I different than other people? Was I different as a child because my mother worked, my parents were divorced, I lived with my grandparents? Will I always be different? Will things always go wrong?

She moves into a new apartment. She has not yet taken out insurance, a fire breaks out, the apartment burns down, she has lost almost everything.

One day, Marcie comes to speak with me holding a small black puppy in her arms. The puppy lies quietly on her lap while we are talking. Her hand rests on the puppy's head, stroking slowly down to the small legs. The tenderness of this gesture passes across Marcie's face, softening it.

Marcie tells me she finds it a great comfort to have the dog with her, at work, in the seat next to her while she is driving. Three months later the dog is run over by a car.

She is a charismatic, celebrated fitness teacher. She has opened a successful aerobics studio. She expands the business, takes on partners, who then take over the business and will no longer allow her to teach in her own studio.

During this time, she meets the man she will soon marry. She and John, his two sons, become the family she wanted as a child. She creates a home for them, built up piece by piece out of childhood longing. These are good years for mother and daughter. Marcie brings me pictures from family dinners. There is elegance, charm, an infectious warmth. At Christmas Lynn arrives at their vacation home in Tahoe at two or three in the morning. The door is thrown open, the dogs stream in and out, she brings homemade cranberry bread, they carry in the tree, the car is loaded with gifts. The family her mother was not able to give Marcie as a child has been created for both of them by the daughter. She hopes for a child of her own; the years pass, she does not get pregnant.

During these years Marcie begins to investigate the causes of her infertility. She has a laparoscopy, a laparotomy, artificial insemination, three in vitro fertilizations. Two of the procedures are successful, then fail during the first weeks. Each means the loss of a child, a dream, a hope, a possibility of ever becoming a mother.

Marcie asks: Is she afraid to inflict her troubled emotional life on a child? Is there something intrinsically wrong with her? Has she been punished by infertility?

Then, just before Lynn's surgery, when Marcie has long since given up hope of having a child, Lynn says to her daughter, "I have a feeling that you will get pregnant and have a child."

A year and a half later, in December, during the last month of Lynn's chemotherapy, I receive an exuberant call. Marcie has become pregnant without trying. During the first weeks of this pregnancy Lynn has a CAT scan. Her colon cancer is in remission. She will live and a grandchild will be born.

We are in the presence of a miracle, a triumph over infertility and death shared equally by mother and daughter.

A few days later Marcie goes in for an ultrasound. The fetal heart has stopped beating.

Marcie's grief for loss of the pregnancy becomes the purified grief of every mother who has lost a child. At moments she is unrecognizable to me, having acquired a poise, a gravity, a stillness. And then the grief breaks through again and I wonder why I have to sit in my chair and can't go over to put my arms around her.

We have been talking together now for more than a decade.

"I still have my mother," she says. "It is having her and you and John that gets me through this."

One month later Lynn's back starts to hurt. The pain is severe and grows worse daily. By the end of the month bone cancer is diagnosed. Lynn is terminal. When Lynn and Marcie come to see me for the second time, Lynn says to her daughter, "I can't understand it. Why did you have that miscarriage? I can't leave you unless you have a daughter to take my place."

Marcie, who has just lost a child, will now also lose a mother. The harshness, cruelty, unpredictability of life are in the room with us. I tell Lynn how much I too have wanted a grandchild, although my daughter is not the marrying kind. The mourning for the unfulfilled settles in easily among the unborn and the dying. It enters quietly into the womanness of our condition, which is never protected for long from grief and loss.

In April, Marcie and Lynn are spending as much time together as possible. Lynn has been going regularly for radiation. Marcie sees her through the nausea, the exhaustion, the loss of appetite, the growing weakness. Marcie is late for her period. We all think it is stress. The doctor won't see her unless they do a pregnancy test. She takes a home pregnancy test, by now routinely. The test is negative. Marcie goes in for more comprehensive tests. Once again, without trying, she is pregnant.

This is the fourth time. And this time, Lynn is dying. For this child to be born it will have to live through its mother's loss of her mother. Will it be the daughter that Lynn has wished for Marcie? Will grandmother live until the child is born?

We have come back to the threshold, the three of us standing at the door to my office. The grandmother is dying. The daughter is pregnant. The story can now move forward.

I stand in the garden to watch them leave. The garden

looks patient, long-suffering, the way it does at midday. Today it is oblivious to the fact that I am about to be lifted up, turned inside out, never put back together the way I had been. If the garden knows Marcie will carry the baby to term, or not, it isn't saying. Mother and daughter are making their way through the gate. They move with terrible caution, Marcie holding the gate wide, standing back awkwardly to let mother pass in front of her. In the next months we will all be tested. Each individually, all three of us together. Mother is moving slowly, stiffly, through that intense late-morning California light, a woman who knows she will die before the year is out.

What will become of the rest of us is unknown. The grandchild who may not be born, the mother-to-be who may not become a mother, the listener who has walked out into the street to see them off. I have seen people drive carefully before. I have never before seen a car move so tenderly away from the curb, so precisely out into the street, so gently into traffic. I would have given a lot to know back then, before I knew how it would all unfold, if it was the passage of death or of death and birth together. But the garden wasn't talking.

• • •

I HAVE TROUBLE with chronology. Even with events that happened recently, only a few months ago, my impressions are not stored in a coherent fashion. Lynn died on July 9, 1994, three months after we met together in my office for the second time. Looking back on those months I see the events in clusters, the repetitive actions caught up together, isolated from the others, which play around them. After or before seems not to matter; I have not been able to register a sequence.

For the sequence, the chronology, I have turned to Marcie. To make a coherent story I need her help. We sit together side by side at my desk, in this room where we have spent so many years face to face across the uncrossable professional distance. Her memory is precise where mine is impressionistic. This makes us useful partners. The text I have given her to read is marked with corrections, suggestions, words circled and noted for their imprecision. My usual heightening is not needed for this story, with its self-contained patterns, its solemn, tragic crossing of the generations.

Marcie and I remind ourselves, we do not dare count on this birth. We remind ourselves, we have work to do. We lean forward, intent on our task. We have a story to tell.

Sometime early in June, Lynn had asked me to visit her at home. She had not been able to keep the many appointments we had made. The pain had been too great, radiation interfered, she had been briefly in the hospital. Now, she had just been told she had six weeks to live.

The next morning, I set out for the first time to visit a client in her own home, unsure of myself, aware of crossing a boundary I have always maintained. During the years of our work, Marcie and I had met for sixty minutes in a formal, confined space, according to an established ritual, which dying has just now overthrown.

So there I am and I am driving through a hot late spring day on an open stretch of freeway without much traffic, and that is the way it will be every time I drive to San Leandro.

Each time I will wonder what I have to give. I will want to turn around and run home and escape the challenge. Each time there will be a fear of facing Lynn's physical decline, the way she might look or smell. And I will, each time, experience a vague, looming, terrifying sense of my sister's dying, some fifty years ago. There will be a sense too of the weighty burden Marcie has taken on, of my own strange role in all this, having promised to help Lynn die when she is ready, having pledged myself to Marcie as a rock, and to myself as someone capable of loving a stranger, to whom I am about to offer more consistency, more availability, more steadiness and strength than I have probably ever been able to offer to anyone in my life.

It seems to be a question of love, that mysterious radiance that caused my arms to grow light. As I drive, this love comes with me; it grows perceptibly as I follow Marcie's directions from Berkeley to San Leandro. Now the core of myself seems deeper than I had imagined, while simultaneously it draws closer to me. It is made of a fierce, uncompromising feeling I remember knowing when I was a child. Because of this love I have become calm, when I would usually be excited. I feel myself to be a steady, knowing, solid presence as I park my car and walk up the driveway to Lynn's house, where Marcie is waiting for me at the door.

A hospital bed has been set up in the family room, doors opening out into a garden above the small town of San Leandro, emerging now from an early morning haze. There are three large dogs; two of them, which I have met before, belong to Marcie. They come in from the deck to meet me at the door. The black dog, Roebie, is wearing a scarf. They come along with me to Lynn's bed, snuffling and nuzzling, getting in one another's way, getting there before me. I have to edge between them to get to Lynn.

And now I am there and after all I am not afraid, although she looks so thin one can imagine her blowing away in the next gust of wind. If work with dying people is (as I now imagine) work I am meant to do, someone has made it very easy for me this first time.

Lynn has not lost any of her beauty. The high cheek-bones, the fine, sculpted arch of her nose in a face that has always been strong, these have only become more percept-ible. I sit down next to her and take her hand. But then I am on my feet again, bending over to embrace her, with that same infinite lightness in my arms, which do not want to cause pain. I have the strongest feeling that I belong here, have brought what is necessary, will not let anyone down, as I have always feared, if I were ever tested, I surely would.

Lynn whispers, "I have been thinking about you." Her voice is soft, husky, so expressive the few words carry an enlarged meaning.

If Lynn is nearly unrecognizable, all the hardness burned away, Marcie has been equally transformed. Her face (wiser, more knowing) seems to have registered the intensity of her concentration on her mother. Every slightest movement, each passing tremor of Lynn's face, the slow, burdened rising up of her knees, the fluttering movement of her hands across the bedcovers, carries a message for Marcie, who responds without hesitation, sure of what must be done. Later on, when Lynn can hardly swallow, when she will no longer be able to say what she needs, Marcie will learn exactly when to feed her water, drop by drop, from a syringe. She is tender, authoritative, determined. I can see exactly the sort of mother she would make.

I take Lynn's hand, this too a repetitive gesture. Lynn's hands are cold, mine equally so. Marcie and I are sitting beside her bed, sometimes silent, sometimes chattering, sometimes talking about Lynn, who hears us, smiles wryly, occasionally comments. I am holding Lynn's right hand between my own, trying to keep the pressure as light as possible. Meanwhile, my hands have begun to grow warm. At first I feel apologetic about this, having noticed a slight redness in my hands, which have always embarrassed me. I don't want to withdraw my touch, or I would certainly slip my hands beneath the folds of my skirt the way I often do, to keep them hidden. Lynn is lying quietly.

She has not drawn up her knees in pain. Therefore I myself grow quiet.

Marcie looks at my hands. I wonder if she finds them extremely ugly. By now it has gone beyond redness, perspiration. My hands are heating up with an intensity that seems to stream out of them into Lynn. Marcie and I exchange a glance, a gesture on my part that amounts to a shrug of my shoulders. Nevertheless, I wouldn't let go if my life depended on it.

This radiant, streaming sensation goes on for a long time, during which I can't take my eyes off Lynn. I feel as if I'd been glued to her, as if there were nothing in life that mattered more than my being here to let this warmth pass through me into her. Then, her left hand begins a slow, toilsome journey across the bed, passes across her body, steadily moving in my direction until our hands, all four of them, are clasped together in a radiant knot.

Because I am afraid of my thoughts I try to keep myself from thinking. Cloud patches of the not quite thought cross the space I am trying to keep empty. I remember the family story about my grandmother and her healing hands. I have heard that my mother, in the wildness of her grief when my sister was dying, took her to faith healers.

This was thought to be a reversion to the ways of the old country. My own hands have always been useless, dropping things, unable to thread needles, tie knots. Now these hands have become knowing, autonomous, indifferent to my confusion. They have found their work, they are getting on with it.

In more focused moments, trying to take stock of what is happening, I feel that I am being hollowed out so that a radiant energy can flow through me into Lynn. This energy does not seem to be mine, it arises elsewhere, seems merely to pass through me, as if Lynn and I were threaded to a mysterious world that works in silence, cannot be named, throws itself open to those who are dying.

Finally, Lynn says, "It's too much," and moves her hands away from mine.

Instantaneously, the heat withdraws from my hands, they start to cool down, lose their redness. Within a few moments they have returned to their usual ice-cold state.

It is very quiet at the bedside, not at all what I had imagined a deathbed would be. The room seems awash in a golden stillness, in which Marcie and I, who have always been formal with each other, now perceptibly relax. Lynn wakes up as I am getting ready to leave. She whispers to me, as I lean down to kiss her good-bye, "I love you."

Marcie says, "What happened before, Ma? Why did you take away your hand? Did you feel something?"

Lynn response, matter-of-factly, "There was too much energy," she says. "I couldn't take any more."

Marcie and I walk outside together. We are standing in front of the door, almost awkwardly. It isn't easy to step out into the street, where my old gray Saab is shimmering through its coating of dirt.

Marcie hugs me good-bye, then she thanks me. She says, "I will send you a check."

We are facing each other. I am caught in one of those moments when I am likely to talk too much because I don't yet know what I am feeling.

"No, no," I say to gain time. Then in a rush: "Could never possibly charge for this. I will come whenever she asks for me."

Marcie considers this. "If you are sure," she says, but I know she knows I am.

She walks with me down the driveway toward my car. John has driven up, the dogs are frisking around us, the street has just turned into a river of dark light and now I wade across it to the old Saab as if I were paddling through a beatitude.

THE WALK ACROSS the room from the door to Lynn's bed is a bobbin on which the weeks of Lynn's dying have been turned. Each time it is the same passage. Each time I have to walk past my sister's dying. Each time, during the slow walk across the room, the dogs coming along the way dogs do, I sense the presence of that unseen world, as if dying made it more available than usual.

When I am not with Lynn I feel that I am connected to her by a fine filament of concentration. Sometimes this feeling becomes so strong I have to sit down on the floor, put my head in my hands to come to terms with it. The days when I was a rational skeptic seem to have ended a long time ago. I can't explain what is happening to me; I am willing to live it out, through all its mystery, if I can wrest from it something of value for Marcie and Lynn.

Marcie and I have agreed. She can call me anytime, as many times a day as she needs me. Lynn and I have agreed. Whenever she wants me to come to sit with her, I will come. My role is largely passive; I wait, I prepare, I gather my resources, I let myself open to whatever unknown powers seem willing to help me. I had wanted to find a vocation, work that would draw me beyond myself. This work has found me. It is Marcie who has the daily work of providing her mother with the most comfortable, best possible dying.

This means cooking her mother's favorite foods so that Lynn can be persuaded to take a bite or two. She has always loved Marcie's cooking. She has no appetite when Marcie isn't there to feed her. Marcie sits next to her making lists of foods. Sometimes, when Lynn has eaten, she has to throw it all up and Marcie has learned how to take care of this, too. If love is intimacy and intimacy involves touch, these two women are more loving, more intimate than ever in their lives before, and this too is the gift wrested from Lynn's dying.

Marcie monitors the medications; there are several, they have to be given in precise amounts at regular times. There is morphine, against pain, in liquid and tablet form. Often Marcie has to guess at the degree of pain when it is difficult for Lynn to communicate. There are suppositories; they are essential to combat nausea but not easy for a daughter to administer. Sometimes, increasingly now, the body cannot regulate its functions. Marcie learns how to lift her mother, use the sheets to turn her, knowing every movement is causing pain, to clean her, to prepare the bed again. She arranges for caretakers, sets up the home hospice visits. I persuade her to take off on the weekends. Marcie has to conserve strength, there is the baby to consider. By now the fetal heartbeat has been heard.

Lynn and Marcie are unrecognizable to me, all three of us not what we were when we began this work together. The expressive love the daughter has always wanted from her, the dying mother is giving, day and night, in response to every gesture of care. By letting Marcie take care of her, by entrusting her dying to her, by leaning on her, as she has never before been willing to do, Lynn knowingly, deliberately, consummates their bond. None of this is easy for Marcie. Still, never once during all those weeks, not once during our countless telephone calls, is Marcie unable to cope. The softening in the mother has been transposed, as it reaches the daughter, into an unaccountable strength, unfailing patience, determination.

Behind the scenes, I find out how to help someone die if they should wish to choose the precise moment of death. This takes research, more research, countless telephone calls, a lot of refusals, endless discussion. My friends think I am taking a big risk. It is against the law for dying people to choose to die, therefore against the law to help them. My New Age spiritual friends think I am not showing reverence for the process of dying. It should, they feel, be lived out fully to the end. My medical friends warn me about botched attempts to help people die.

There are many ways to die voluntarily. The solutions, as they are presented, all involve risk or impossibility. If I can locate, somehow, the drugs Lynn would need there is no guarantee she will be able to swallow them. She is already scarcely able to get down a few mouthfuls of food. The drugs, even in large amounts, even if they could be swallowed, may not be sufficient. Supplemental injections may be required. But how to obtain what would need to be injected? Marcie and I practice with plastic bags. We want to see what it might be like to slip one over one's head, but we all find this solution, which is said to be entirely reliable, unacceptable.

I am convinced Lynn must be given assurance that she is not out of control. She has lived by will and self-determination. It is essential, I feel, that she be able to call upon these while she is dying. She has to know the pain cannot grow too great, the suffering not become overwhelming, that her dying will not be prolonged indefinitely while Marcie suffers the burden. Then, reassured that she has the choice to die, I do not think she will exercise it. My role is to make this choice possible. Making it possible has become a sacred obligation.

It is easy to see why I began to think of this work as spiritual. It took longer to discover the trajectory by which it became political. At the time, consequences, movements, issues, struggles in the social world were far from my thoughts. Still, from the moment I agreed to help Lynn die, this promise drew the social world in upon us. A personal response to an intimate request, made from one woman to another, in the privacy of a consultation room, had a political resonance.

Here, the heart and the law stand in opposition, a fact that by itself made my work with Lynn political. Even in its most private gesture, this work raised questions of self-determination, the state's right to intervene in private acts, an individual's right to choose her own way of living and dying. As soon as I began to work with Lynn, I also began to notice how poorly most people die, lonely, terrified, without guidance, hampered by laws that intrude upon this act in which one would imagine our freedom should be as unfettered as dying allows.

While Lynn was dying, two of my clients had observed people close to them die of cancer. These deaths were harsh, unforgiving, angry, spiritually unsupported, and in one case, medically speaking, the patient was seriously deprived. For people without insurance or adequate income, home hospice care is unavailable, as is hospitalization and adequate medication to deal with pain. There are one or two grassroots organizations that train people to work with the dying. The training is itself hampered by laws that prevent people unlicensed by the state from using "psychological tools" or doing "therapy." Many doctors, when approached, were afraid to prescribe the medications their patients would have needed to end their lives. The search for medications to help the dying die therefore leads to the drug underground, where 50 percent of the barbiturates manufactured in this country eventually show up. Conversations about these matters are uncomfortable by telephone. In one case, a prescription, in triplicate copies, was eventually obtained, but most pharmacies did not stock the medication, the prescription was good only for one week, and by the time a pharmacy was located that would be willing to order the medication, the prescription had run out and the doctor was now reluctant to write another.

The possibility of assisting Lynn suggested the possibility of helping others, getting additional training for myself, helping to train others. While intently absorbed in one woman's illness, I had become fully engaged in the world.

One day, Marcie and Lynn and I, together at Lynn's bed, pass back and forth between us the first cloudy picture of the inner world of Marcie's body. The sonogram makes many things clear. The baby is thriving, she is a girl, she has gone on living while her grandmother is dying.

Then, a few days later, I am able to give Lynn the assurance that we know how to help her die, we have the means to do it, she has only to say the word, the choice of life and death is in her hands.

LYNN LEANS ON Marcie, Marcie on me, I on an unknown world from which I have begun to receive the assurance that dying, whether or not an ending, is not to be feared.

Because I know this (whatever knowing means), I now have something of great value to offer Lynn, if she believes me.

I anguish over this "knowledge" during my drive, that singular, sunlit slow passage from home to deathbed. But when I get there, when I have embarked from the threshold with the dogs, by the time I reach Lynn's bed, I am prepared to take any risk to tell her what I think I know.

I mumble the words. "I have been thinking about you all weekend," I say.

She struggles to answer, manages a low, rasping voice: "I have been thinking about you too."

"I felt so much love for you.

She nods, knowingly. "I too," she says. "So much love."

"I was walking in the woods up at Point Reyes. I felt very close to you, almost as if I were sitting here with you or you had come with me. It's hard to explain."

"I know," she says.

"I wish I could tell you what I have understood. It's all here inside me. It's hard to bring out."

She says, matter-of-factly, "Your presence brings it."

Lynn is still beautiful. She is always freshly bathed, in beautifully laundered nightgowns. She knows dying is not a pleasant business. She has taken pains to make herself presentable. She has been told she has less than a month to live. Nevertheless, she has her hair cut and permed, her arms waxed, she gets a manicure. Flowers fill the room, the rugs have been cleaned. She intends to leave everything in order and wants her dying to be tolerable for the rest of us.

She has been saying good-bye to friends and relatives. The farewells pass through Marcie, who has become the containing vessel for all stress, all emotion. She sees people in and out, tells them when it is time to go, tirelessly adjusts the pillows, the blankets, opens and closes the windows, regulates the flow of warmth, air, light.

The visits exhaust Lynn; she is easily agitated, she often needs quiet, although Marcie makes sure the family is always present, the dogs roaming about, barking sometimes, chewing at one another, pouncing, picking up toys, getting into a tug of war. Marcie has broken the great divide that separates the living from the dying.

As words begin to be more difficult for Lynn, as it becomes hard for her to make physical gestures, her eyes take over the burden of communication. In Lynn's gaunt face, the blue-gray eyes live with an enhanced vitality. I have her hand in mine, the same radiant intensity is heating up again and passing between us. This time I am less embarrassed about my red hands, glad I have something tangible to offer Lynn as I sit next to the deathbed beside Marcie, who observes what is happening, silently.

I have never spoken to Lynn about my wish to find a life of service. Now I want to tell her how I am discovering this life, through her. I want her to know that her dying has brought me an incomparable gift. It has placed me squarely in relation to a world that has before now lightly touched, then invariably eluded me. If hands could talk, if this warmth had a voice, Lynn would already know the uneasy wonder I feel at this transformation.

I have glimpsed the tiny illuminations, the whole sequence of awakenings, by which my spiritual life has been pieced together since I was a small child. Each awakening, followed by a deep sleep, each new illumination followed by a forgetting. These isolated, singular events now seem connected to one another, a sequence of transformational steps leading to this very moment. I want Lynn to know about this, but the impressions pass so quickly language cannot hitch itself to them. I think she would also understand my sadness, which now suddenly has become acute, that there will probably never be a grandchild to whom I can hand down these fragments of vision. A dense sorrow, familiar, almost impersonal, seems to grow up between Lynn and me, along the line of connection where our hands meet. Is this Lynn's sorrow because she will die before her grandchild will be born? My sorrow because I cannot tell her what I so desperately want her to know? A shared sorrow because Lynn and I met too late, then came together in this high, exacting drama where we have only the most momentous gifts to exchange?

Just then, Lynn looks at me fixedly. She says, with that apparent effort that brings a marked solemnity into all her words, because they cost her so much to speak them, "Kim, I know you have wanted a grandchild. I know your daughter doesn't want to have children. I'm not going to be here when my grandchild is born. I want to give you my grandchild."

Lynn is gazing curiously at me. I am trying to figure out if unspoken thoughts flow easily between one person and another when dying has revoked the illusion of boundaries.

"What if she doesn't want to have the responsibility, Ma?" Marcie admonishes her, gently.

But Lynn is having this conversation with me. "I know," she says, "you have always been here for Marcie. I am leaving her in your hands. I know you will look out for her."

"Ma," Marcie says, "what if Kim . . ."

But now I manage to say, through the anguish I feel, because I know words cannot deliver the assurance for which she is asking, "I will always look out for her," while Lynn nods once, then closes her eyes.

She has given me her daughter and granddaughter. I have received them. And then, as Lynn settles back against the pillow my hands get so hot I am afraid they are going to burn her.

The next morning, Lynn wakes up and asks Marcie to prepare a meal for her. She eats pasta, squash with butter, a quesadilla Marcie prepares. The following day it is fish, potato, snap peas, salad. Lynn asks for an éclair. Marcie brings one. For two days Lynn is fully awake, full of her wry, resigned, ironic humor, telling everyone she has it in mind to get up out of that bed and let them deal with the dying.

She doesn't leave. She becomes weak again, and says things people don't understand. One day she says to me, "I haven't been here for years."

"Is it a good place?" I ask.

"Oh yes, yes," she murmurs and then she goes back to the hard business of dying.

A day or two later she wakes up; with perfect clarity she asks Marcie to send for me. Then, very deliberately, she turns to everyone present to ask if they agree to this. But why would she suddenly need their permission?

Then, on the drive to San Leandro, I remember my pledge to help Lynn die. Has the time come when the pledge will be called in?

When I arrive, Lynn says she wants to have me sit there with her, silently. I want this too and take her hands. The silence runs deep. I understand that I am there to help her die, not with plastic bags or injections, but through some quality of my presence. What quality?

Lynn seems far away from us but her pulse is still strong. We all know dying can go on and on and that Lynn hadn't wanted this. John and Marcie are standing together at the foot of the bed.

"I don't know how I know this," I tell Lynn. "But I am here to help you die. Although to tell you the truth I haven't a clue how to do it."

Far, far away, a ghostly smile; then, to reassure me, a firm pressure against my hands.

Four days later, on a hot Saturday morning in July, I know I have to go to Lynn. This time, for the first time urgently, I make my way through the sunlit passage, drive up to the house, cross the threshold, get past the dogs, arrive at the deathbed.

Lynn has developed a high fever. When I take her hands, hers are burning. There are beads of sweat on her forehead and lips. Marcie and I sit across from each other, on opposite sides of the bed. We both watch my hands, then my arms, all the way up to my elbow, become swollen and red, as if I am actively drawing the fever out of Lynn. Very gradually, over the next few hours, this troubled heat of living and dying passes into me, then through me as Lynn begins to cool down.

First it is her hands, which are becoming ice cold. Her

feet had been feverish. Now, when Marcie touches them, they too have turned cold and somewhat blue. We see a fine line of pale shadow form around Lynn's lips; we had been told by the hospice nurse that this rim of paleness would appear before death.

Lynn's eyes are wide open, her head turned toward me, the enormous, piercing gaze fixed on me. But there is almost no face left so these eyes seem to be staring out from a sharp bone structure that has already become a skeleton. I feel that the gaze is not easy to hold. I am looking straight at death. A crust forms on her lips; Marcie gently wipes it away. Lynn's breathing is labored. She closes her eyes, I put my head close to her ear. I keep murmuring, "We have shared a very great love. Rest in this love. I will come with you as far as I can. You are not alone."

This murmuring goes on for a long time. Then, the fever seems to enter me with a sudden rush. The swelling in my arms rises up all the way to my shoulders and Lynn grows colder and colder and then I am exhausted and don't want to leave but Marcie is worried about me. "You have taken care of me for all these years," she says. "Now I have to take care of you."

Lynn dies three hours later, while Renate and I are sitting in a cafe, talking about my sister's death.

Since then, the grandchild Lynn gave me has had another sonogram picture taken. She sucks her thumb, curls up in a ball, has well-formed arms and legs and tiny perfect fingers.

Three

ROOT AND BRANCH

*S*tories require a listener who can suspend disbelief long enough to let the tale emerge. Once under way, the story will take care of itself, gather momentum, forget about the listener, charge off on its mission, whether well received or even vaguely comprehended. Beginnings are the problem.

So there we are, my father and I, cutting back the ivy that grows over the rickety fence from the neighbor's garden. In this imaginary world, my mother does not have Alzheimer's, my father is not dead. Our house in Los Angeles has not been sold. I can still go down for a weekend, find my childhood room as it used to be. I can go outside to work with my father in his garden. It is getting late. My mother would be coming home from work, rushing in the way she always used to so that we could have dinner before she rushed out again for a meeting. We would take off our gardening gloves, pack away our trowel and rake, and go out front to meet her, to help her carry in the stacks of pamphlets, brochures, leaflets to be stored in the garage.

It is not conceivable that I would have just said to my father, "You know, Dad, the world is in such a terrible state I don't think the human race can survive unless we learn to bring our lives into harmony with an unseen, spiritual world." But that is what I want to say.

If I said to my father that teachers were sent to us at particular moments of historic urgency, when the human community seemed to be at a loss, my father would be constrained to ask, Sent by whom?

This is a reasonable question; my father would not have been satisfied by an answer that evaded it. If we were out working together in the garden (if we were out working together in the garden!) and I were to say to him, I accept the teachers, their presence and their mission, although I do not know anything about the mechanism by which they were sent, my father would have shaken his head, sadly. He would have been greatly disappointed in his daughter.

As poetry, fable, legendary tale, my father would have received these notions patiently. He would have said, "Did I ever tell you about that man in Moscow who believed he could communicate with birds?" But I would not have been able to tell my father that I took these ideas seriously.

SEVERAL YEARS BEFORE my father died, he and I were at the dining room table, after dinner. I was reading the *Tao Te Ching* in a paperback edition with a smiling, wise old fat man on the cover. I don't know how the book happened to end up in full view, since I usually kept it hidden, feeling that it was a subversive text, Taoist, mystical, inclined to quietism. My father opened the book, came to a marked passage, read it aloud. "To retire when the task is accomplished is the way of heaven."

I used to have a habit of leaning way back in my chair until the chair touched the wall. I did this whenever I was nervous or excited. Whenever I did this my father would say, "You know what happens to people who lean back in chairs? Where do they end up? On the floor."

And I would say, "Yes, Daddy," in a tone of infinite resignation but not put my chair back where it belonged.

This time he said, "What do you suppose this means?"

"It means,"—I was young then, and I always knew what things meant—"there is no point struggling against the nature of the moment. You do what you have to do, then step back. If the time isn't right there's no point in fighting."

"Is this something you believe?" my father asked.

"It means human destiny is guided by the ways of heaven."

My father gazed at me, a look on his face of weighing, considering. "When I was young, it was a liberation for us to no longer believe in heaven. We thought the ways of heaven unjust, unreliable. We believed instead in man's capacity to change the world."

"It hasn't exactly happened the way you might have imagined."

"That's true, that's true," he said, lowering his voice as if he would have preferred that my mother not overhear this conversation.

"So this book is of interest to you," he went on after a long silence. "If you are finished with it for now, I will read it."

Did he read it? Memory does not say. Was I leaving the next day, the conversation therefore forever postponed?

I still have the book with its yellow cover, the curved moon-smile of the bald fat man, his ears curled with a delicious wisdom. Memory has ended abruptly. Did my father disappoint me? What in the world would he have said?

Perhaps he gave me back the book silently, the next morning at breakfast. Maybe he was about to say something when my mother bustled in and the book disappeared from the dining room table, fast. Did we exchange a glance, my father and I, as if we shared a terrible secret? Did that quick glance promise me a hearing some day when the time was right? That was thirty years ago. Is this the time? Shall I go ahead and risk it?

IT MIGHT BE best to begin this tale by talking to my father about my client Nadine. She is a visionary painter, a French Jew whose family came badly through the Second World War. Some time ago, during our regular session, she began talking about a woman named Meera, who lives in Germany. Meera gives *darshan*, a blessing to those who come to sit with her, four nights a week, in all seasons, in an obscure German village near Frankfurt. Some two hundred people are present on these occasions. They come from all over the world, although Meera has never allowed publicity for these sittings. Silently, in a deep meditative concentration, Meera places her hands on both sides of a devotee's head, removes her hands, gazes into the devotee's eyes. Nadine felt that she had been transported into a deep silence, unlike any silence she had known before.

I was listening to all this sympathetically, although with some skepticism. Meera's followers believe that she is an embodiment of the Hindu divine mother. That is why her devotees refer to her as Mother Meera.

I am able to imagine god in a female form. But a woman with the power to open a path to the divine simply by looking into a devotee's eyes? God embodied? Here on earth, now? In this very moment, while Nadine and I are in conversation?

Of course, my skepticism is irrelevant, it cannot do justice to Nadine's experience. To know her, I have to enter into her own sense of meaning. If she has lived through an event different from any I have known, the appropriate response is curiosity. Well then, I am curious: I want to know more about her experience, to draw closer to it, without judgment.

I note this state of mind: I wanted to know more, without judgment.

The next time we met, Nadine brought in a book written by a man who had worked with Mother Meera. I was worried when I first received the book. How interested was I? How open would I be? I knew from the first paragraphs that I was in the hands of a fine writer. He was describing his childhood in India. I left my own life to join him there. I felt the book was speaking directly to me, with a message I had long been expected, although I had not realized I had been waiting for it.

Psychologically speaking, this excitement, my fascination with the figure of Mother Meera, my sense of her special relevance to me might have meant I had opened myself to my client's experience so that I could understand it through my own. Similarly, I might be experiencing what is called a projective identification; my client may have needed to relocate her experience of faith and doubt in me, so that I could work it over for her and return it to her in an altered form. Or, my work with her over the last months may have awakened a strong, personal response to her, so that I wanted to merge with her experience, to bring about a greater closeness between us. But of course it was equally possible that my client was affecting me as profoundly as our work together was influencing her. Perhaps, in deciding to work with her when my schedule seemed already complete, in offering her a reduced fee because I had liked her paintings of wild animals, snakes, goddesses, dancing worshipers, I had responded to her capacity to change me. Our work together was based on a strong kinship and personal affinity; we had liked each other the minute we met, had entrusted ourselves to this work for that reason. Perhaps we had been "brought together" (as Nadine might say) to become teachers for each other on a shared spiritual path.

How would I place these events in relation to Marcie's mother? Did I become interested in Meera because I had promised to help a woman die and had no idea how this was to be accomplished? Certainly, death and dying were on my mind when Nadine first told me about Mother Meera.

Meera's story is the story of three people. There is her uncle, Mr. Reddy, who had traveled all over India since he was a young man, looking for the mother. There is Adilak-shmi, a highly educated young Indian woman who suddenly got on a train one day, leaving her family and a life of privilege, to search for the mother. And there is Meera, a young girl living in Mr. Reddy's home, a niece or distant relative whom he had not known, but then immediately recognized as the divine mother for whom, all his life, he had been seeking.

I was disarmed by these gentle people who searched for god, who had known since childhood that their lives would have no meaning unless they found her. I found their stories wistfully compelling, as if I shared a bond with them I would otherwise never have confessed to myself. Perhaps if I had been born in their culture, I too would be able to imagine that gods walked the streets, visited one in dreams, could be met after a long absence in one's own home, in the form of a young girl who, since childhood, had talked about "going to various lights."

The gods I knew about, even the great mother, seemed far off, abstract, hypothetical. Sometimes I thought about them as archetypal images that belonged to the psyche. When I felt a wish to worship nature, I imagined I had projected onto a solitary tree a luminous cloud configuration, a sense of divinity that streamed from the human heart. I am a Western intellectual. It puzzled me that the story of Adilakshmi and Mr. Reddy seemed so plausible, agreeable, sweetly engaging. I never once thought they were mad, or that Meera was a deluded young woman with a charismatic schizophrenic personality. I liked them, they seemed wholesome to me and well intentioned and I wanted Renate to read all about them.

The book's author, Andrew Harvey, had met up with the three of them as a young man, on one of his trips to India. The book was an account of his visionary experience with Meera, whom he had come to love and worship as the divine mother. Harvey was a college professor, the youngest fellow ever elected to a college at Oxford, as the book jacket informed me. It was easy enough to identify with him, a gay man, often in despair about his relationships, an intellectual living out the bleakness of late-twentieth-century intellectual life. But then again, he was also a seeker who kept taking off to faraway places. He'd been in Tibet, at various ashrams in India; he meditated, read sacred books, then encountered Mother Meera.

As for me, I had never admitted to myself that I was interested in finding a teacher or a spiritual master. I had never wanted to live in an ashram, although I had spent a brief time as a student in Tassahara, the Zen meditation center in the Santa Cruz mountains. At that time in my life, when I knew I had to go somewhere, it came down to a choice between a monastery and a kibbutz. I chose the kibbutz; I went to Israel.

IN MY DREAMS, my father has a way of coming back from the dead wearing his old leather jacket. Sometimes he wears the yellow sweater his mother had knit for him because he was leaving home to go to MIT. This jacket, this yellow sweater had lasted thirty years and were part of my childhood.

Maybe my father has been coming back from the dead to hear this story. Maybe, having been dead, he is no longer skeptical about unseen worlds or mysterious communications. In one of my dreams I threw my arms around him to tell him how well he looked. Then I felt embarrassed. How well he looked? The man was dead!

I used to love the way my father listened. He didn't fidget or smoke or toy with a spoon. Sometimes he stroked his mustache, a contemplative gesture. Nevertheless, this story is about to get much harder to tell him, even if he has come back to hear it. It involves some extravagant emotion, certain devotional gestures that embarrass me. But here we go:

Renate and I went for a walk in Abbott's Lagoon.

There is a narrow sandy path that leads down past the lagoon to the open sea, cows grazing in the pasture to our right, a distant cluster of white farm buildings on a slight rise to our left, in that long, evocative, strangely disturbing mystical light of west Marin.

We weren't talking much, both caught by the sudden, sacred beauty of the place. It took on, as we walked, a majestic stillness. Even the birds flitting over the high grass, the quail scurrying across the path in front of us, the jackrabbit keeping a steady distance ahead of us seemed transfixed, as if we were the only creatures moving and breathing against this painted backdrop, charged with presence.

Suddenly I wanted to bury my face in my hands. I felt that I was becoming very small in the presence of something wondrous. I also felt childlike, full of joy and excitement. I felt no need to keep my experience hidden from Renate, although with anyone else I would have felt cautious, wary, as if I were opening myself to potential ridicule.

I said, "I want to fall on my knees."

Renate said, "The body wants to do something in response to so much feeling."

The same night, in the living room on the couch in front of the fire, I told Renate that Andrew Harvey's experience was familiar to me, that I recognized the journey, the transformation, the awakening through light. I had known this journey years ago, but had "forgotten" it. The facts had remained, but now they filled up again with meaning. Mother Meera seemed authentic, believable, an important teacher, perhaps something more. I must have said this wistfully, in the spell of the book. It seemed to tell a legendary tale of remote events in distant centuries.

"But that is a child's wish for a divine mother," Renate says thoughtfully as she adds a log to the fire.

"Maybe, maybe not. Maybe children know things we have forgotten. Maybe they live in the real world and that is why it seems magical to them. Maybe what we have experienced today is a miracle and we are too stubborn to recognize it for what it is."

"Why call it a miracle? Why not take it simply for what it is?

"What is it?"

"Seeing. Recognizing. Taking the time to look. Noticing. Maybe Abbott's Lagoon is always that beautiful and we ignore it and today we didn't."

"That's what I mean by a miracle."

During breakfast, on the deck, out among the trees, the next day, we talked about how rarely we had ever spoken together about "these experiences." They seemed to belong to a shy, hidden part of the self that did not confess itself even to a trusted lover. For the first time in all these years (almost ten years now) I told Renate how much my younger life had been influenced by "these experiences." Of course, she had read my story about light pouring down in the mountain valley in Ireland, my vision of the dancing goddess. But writing, this most private of acts, even when later it becomes public, is safer than saying some things out loud, directly to another person. When spoken, one feels committed to the words, they become part of the relationship one is building up with another person, there's nowhere to hide, no distance: there you are, over breakfast, swallowing a bit of oat scone to tell someone you love that you want to give your life in service to the world, you are looking for a way to offer yourself, you are a mystic.

We were out on the deck, under the trees, for a long time. Renate, more skeptical, more hesitant than I when it comes to handing herself over to "excitement," reminded me that we once were quite close to the divine feminine.

When we first met we had been involved in the women's spirituality movement, "praying" in our own way with poems and songs we made up when we were out for walks. Little by little our playful reverence had been abandoned. Psychology took over, we were in therapy, we both went back to graduate school. Her therapist had thought of our rituals as "children's games." Mine had thought the "presence" I felt in nature was the return of a childhood fantasy.

Many people we know would find these matters nothing special, certainly nothing that would require hushed voices. But for us, apparently, questions of spiritual awareness, realization, enlightenment, transformative inner experience, sensitivity to the consciousness of nature had been thoroughly whitewashed with plausible, rational, psychological explanations.

"We've been here before," Renate said. "What's the big leap from saying the feminine divine principle is embodied in all of us to saying it's embodied in Mother Meera?"

"We say it, but do we really mean it? It's a fanciful notion for us, whimsical, appealing. Meera has called our bluff. We never took literally the idea of the divine feminine. Now, a woman says, 'I AM the divine feminine, I am the mother embodied,' and we are right back in our skeptical stance, scoffing, incredulous, disbelieving."

I MIGHT GO look for my father in the garden. He would be interested in the small, tamed world Renate has built up out of our own private wilderness. He would recognize the homesickness for Europe that created the stone patio with its small fountain, where passionflowers are growing. He, I know, would shake his head (marveling about the weather), the way he did in Los Angeles in the late fall after twenty years there. He would hang his shirt from the clothesline to work bare-chested among his roses. My father would be at home in Renate's garden, where the skeptical is hard at work raking about through the sacred.

And I, have I replaced my father's secret garden with another?

But if I go out to the garden I will not find him, not even in the garden of my imaginary world where people come back from the dead. My story has lost him. He would not understand the idea I am trying to work out when I wonder if, against all rational persuasion, I take seriously a young Indian woman living in Germany who says she is here to aid in the transformation and evolution of the world, through the power of divine light, called in Hindu the light of Paramatman, the supreme being.

My father might share the view that the world is in serious trouble, we are passing through a profound social and ecological crisis, the issue is grave, even apocalyptic. He would be able to make nothing, I imagine, of the widespread New Age idea that spiritual help is being sent to us through dreams and visions, in sudden awakenings, by the presence here of teachers and masters. If he can make nothing of this, how can his daughter? In telling this story to my father, I have staged a dialogue between the old left, to which I have belonged from birth, and a new age in which I cannot locate myself.

But why not? The recognition of nature as the home of the divine, the celebration of the human body as the true celestial city marks New Age and particularly women's spirituality with a highly distinctive message. Subjective knowledge of the divine is now available on every street corner and in domestic gardens. Is it really true that my father would not be interested in any of this?

Not that my father would ever walk out on me. If I told him I had fallen in love with a fascist or decided to exploit the workers to become a millionaire, he would have been shocked. But he would not have left the room. It is I who cannot keep him here next to me as I urge myself forward step by step through these difficult thoughts.

Therefore I am alone at my desk and, believe me, it is lonely. I sit quietly assembling words. They gather to a force of twofold disloyalty, against my father and against Renate. Just to think these thoughts, merely to entertain them seriously; not to think them true, only to imagine they might be true, has the potential to disrupt my life. If divine work is being done, if help is being given, if each of us has some small, relevant part to play, I will try to play mine, no matter the cost.

A suspense has entered my relationship with Renate. It would fall to pieces if she follows me against her own desires; it won't last if what I am about to do cannot include her. We might wish it to be otherwise, make resolutions, promises, commitments to each other; in the end we would be drawn apart because the paths of our individual development no longer coincided. This is harsh; it has happened to both of us before.

It also happened with my father. To reach him on some common ground I am forced back beyond memory to the time when he was growing up in an Orthodox Jewish family, therefore must have had a bar mitzvah, therefore must have known Hebrew. None of this was ever mentioned in our home. Such history was actively ignored, so that I have had to put it together piece by piece over the years. I knew he and his brothers sat together at the end of the long Passover table reading and chanting, while the rest of us fiddled about in our secular way. But I never said to myself, My father knows Hebrew. Because I did not think of him as knowing Hebrew I did not wonder how he learned it. It never occurred to me he would have gone to synagogue as a young boy because I had never been in a synagogue. Was he devout, a believer, a dreamy boy with mystical yearnings? I know he was shy. That story he told me. His sister Rose dressed him up when he was small and put him in the front window so that everyone could see her beautiful brother. He hated that story. He hated to be on view. He hid under the bed and refused to come out. Sometimes he smiled his hidden smile when he told this story. He had struggled with shyness all his life.

Does a knowledge of Hebrew prove a bar mitzvah? Does a bar mitzvah mean belief in the divine? Maybe my father was once devout, went through a period of crisis as he broke with his family's ways, left religion behind him when he became a communist, then passed on to his daughter a disposition to feel sensitively where matters of the spirit are concerned.

Jews have an ancient ceremony called *Havdalah*. *Havdalah*, which means "division" or "separation," takes place after nightfall at the end of the Sabbath. The *Havdalah* is said over a cup of wine, with additional benedictions spoken for *besamim*, the fragrant herbs, and for *nerot*, the candles. We never observed this ceremony in our house because we never observed the Sabbath. But my father must have participated in this ceremony at the end of every Sabbath until he left home for MIT.

In the Jewish mystical tradition it is said that on the Sabbath "a queenly visitor entered even the humblest abode, which, due to her presence, was transformed into a royal palace, with the table set, the candles burning and the wine waiting." This queenly visitor was identical with Shekinah, the "feminine, visible, audible manifestation of God's presence on earth." I don't know how many people around the Sabbath table today believe that God, embodied in female form, has been with them on the Sabbath.

But the *Havdalah* marks her departure. Therefore, a box of fragrant spices is passed from hand to hand, to revive the human spirit suffering from the separation.

I feel sure my father had never read the Zohar, the book of light, or any of the cabalist texts. On the other hand, why am I so sure? He was a reader, a scholar, a student of obscure matters. He knew Hebrew, went regularly to synagogue, likely had a bar mitzvah, and celebrated the Sabbath. If he recited prayers and blessings with his family, their meaning and origin would have been likely to interest him in the years before he became a socialist and left it all behind.

On the occasions in childhood when I went out to the garden when my father was there, he would pick up a few herbs, crush them in his hand, offer them to me to smell. It isn't much evidence, I know; it's a fairly common gesture, and it used to irritate me when I wanted only to play with my dog.

When my sister was ten years old she wrote a series of poems in a notebook with a wood cover. She wrote nature poems, to the seasons. They all have a rapturous, worshipful feel to them, as in the line: "I bow my head in gratitude to you, Oh winter. To you."

The spring poem has a psalmic quality to it, although I am certain my sister never read the Psalms. "Arise ye stately trees / Lift up your branches to the sunlight / Lift them up higher, higher, and higher / Lift them with all your might . . . Awaken! Awaken!"

I was not yet born when these poems were written. I don't know if my sister read them to me a few years later. Then everyone in the family had a nightly assignment to read to me before I feel asleep. The autumn poem is more conventionally elegiac. "Down to the earth, leaves / of all color, come / fluttering down. / Red and brown, and golden and yellow / all the world is like a soft-playing cello."

Five years after writing these words she died in late September. By then, my sister's poetic sensibility had changed dramatically. The nature poems had vanished, political poems had taken their place. The one written on February 28, 1940, a few months before I was born, is to Poor Jo the Indian. It documents the white man's stealing of Poor Jo's land. There is also a long narrative poem on lynchings and the poll tax, in which a black man defies the sign that says, "Niggers can't vote here!" The poem ends abruptly: "They strung him up there, nice and high, and let him [illegible] at the sun / Before . . ."

The situation she was trying to describe must have gone beyond a child's imagination.

My sister and my father are both dead. I cannot ask them whether a deep spiritual sensibility lay buried at the heart of our family life. Certainly, it would seem that my mother, the tough one, could not be explained in spiritual terms. Yet, as she aged, her love for the people often made her weep with outrage when she came across an example of injustice. In a language she would never have used, my mother might have been said to suffer from compassion.

A few years ago, when she was ninety years old, when language had largely deserted her, my mother uttered only primal sounds, attempting to communicate with me but now, after a lifetime of eloquence, vainly.

Whenever I went to visit I used to babble along with her. People in her nursing home thought we were conversing together, as perhaps we were. My mother would come out of her enormous solitary babbling distance, awaken the world, spot me or a me she recognized as familiar, smile, let tears run down her cheeks, excitedly repeating, "Snyap, chamsk, chorkum, vwiebetsk," as I babbled back at her. But one day briefly the babbling stopped. My mother looked over at me with a still, searing gaze and said, with perfect clarity, what amounts to her life's credo.

I call Renate to witness; she was there. Otherwise one might suppose this one more of my desperate efforts to hook myself back into my family through shared qualities of love, devotion, compassion, lifelong dedication to a purpose larger than ourselves. We had heard my mother say, "The people," and then repeat again these last clear words we would ever hear her speak: "The people."

I'VE DONE IT, I've roped them in, I've got them all here with me at my desk. Here, it is possible to unearth the hidden core of a person you know so well you wouldn't easily imagine anything could have remained hidden. In trotting out into the forbidden spiritual dimension I am not (it would seem) radically driving off from my family's values, but am driving their political concern back to an essential ground. This may be only a convenient fiction, but it has worked. I am saying what I have to say, they are witnessing. The little girl who bowed her head to winter, brooded about the stealing of Indian land and the lynching of Negroes, the old woman who cried out her final devotions, the man who gardened as if he were at prayer! Back beyond rationality, materialism, atheism, we are a family of devout passions.

Still, I wonder if atheists used to feel shamefaced when they were emerging out of the nineteenth century. Did they feel embarrassed about themselves, as if they were carrying a terrible secret, would be laughed at or pilloried if anyone knew? Probably they felt dangerous and proud, as my father must have felt when he moved to New York and became a communist.

I want to scurry away and hide these papers in the empty space under my bed. How am I going to tell my friends what I am writing? What if Michael says, when he comes back from France, So, what have you been working on all summer? (And of course that is exactly what he will say.)

"Oh, nothing. Just a little book about my love of the divine mother. In her embodied form, of course."

Are we responsible for the things we think? Thoughts can be as involuntary as feelings. Sometimes they are the cognitive expression of profound emotional states, themselves linked to nature and the body as intimately as seasons of hunger or thirst. If one day I start to questions my family's most basic teaching, its secular humanist pride in the abilities of human beings to work out rational solutions to social problems; if I dare to wonder if we, left on our own without the help of the divine, are capable only of destroying ourselves, must I blame myself for these thoughts? They have grown up mysteriously, in darkness, out of unknowing and disbelief. There are many explanations one could give for them, but I am tired of explanations. They are thoughts born of ecstasy; ecstasy has been their teacher.

During the time Lynn was dying, Renate and I frequently went out to spend a weekend at Point Reyes. One day, while we were walking in the woods, Renate reminded me of a dream she had told me about. In her dream I had gone off with a woman spiritual teacher, a master. At the time (many weeks before I had heard of Mother Meera), we had not paid much attention to the dream. But now Renate was upset. Was I about to take off on a new path, breaking with everything in the present, leaving everything behind, to follow this new enthusiasm for Mother Meera? Would I become obsessed, the way I do, talk of nothing else, want her to join me in this experience?

I too had a fear: it seemed to me I was suddenly irresistibly becoming something I had always tried not to be. What if Renate did not like what I was becoming? What if I didn't like her dislike for me?

Every time I went outside, I had a sense of a luminous presence. Feelings, exaltations seem to flow through me, fastening on to this and that. I had the impression that the divine was trying to attract our attention. As we walked, I kept pulling Renate by the arm, pointing out a white branch, a ragged bit of lichen, the sudden revelation of a solitude of herons. It was true: I had become a formidable pest.

But for me, these thoughts were themselves a rapture. They didn't grow up easily, they had to overcome an enormous pressure of scoffing and doubt. But when they arrived, full-blown, flourishing, the joy they brought was indescribable, and for a time the bleak sense of doubting everything vanished. I had become a believer. Oh, a believer, but in what?

That night, falling asleep, I was aware of a growing conviction: I've found my way again. My direction has been established. I'm not wandering, searching, I'm pointed to where I must go. (Had I been wandering, searching?) Around this sense of direction I compose myself. The pattern of myself has been revealed. This is who I am: I am a lover of the mother, of god. What matters to me is this love, this relation, the need to serve in the name of this love, to work in the world so that I am addressing its crisis, its turmoil, its despair.

Exalted moods of this kind, which are, in one form or another, quite familiar to me, would be routinely regarded by some people as manic states, conditions one had better (all things considered) do one's best to rein in.

Is that what Renate was worrying about?

Sunday afternoon, walking back from the beach, fog coming in, a sense of desolation, as if the light that teaches seeing had been wiped out. We both felt it. We said nothing about our future, the trips we might make or not make to Germany, alone or together. I wondered aloud if this is how it felt—bleak, desolate—when one could not believe in the existence of the divine.

THERE IS SOMETHING about the relationship between guru and disciple, master and devotee that causes many people to feel a shade uncomfortable. I have always been one of them. So much surrender of individual will to the superior knowing of another person—this tends to run against the grain of our democratic educations. Nevertheless, anyone on a spiritual path soon becomes familiar with the great couples of the spiritual traditions. (I myself have recently become fascinated with the relationship between Rumi and Shams, Castaneda and Don Juan, Irena Tweedie and her Teacher, Reshad Field and Hamid, Sweet Mother and Aurobindo, Sri Yukteswar and Paramahansa Yogananda.) Usually, it is the disciple who brings the teacher to the world's attention through his writing, whether in love poems (Rumi) of great intensity or through personal accounts of transformation (Castaneda). The relationship of Andrew Harvey with Mother Meera clearly belonged to this line.

But what fascinated me?

There are many elements of this story that make for a great, legendary tale. A young man learning from an even younger woman; an Oxford fellow devoting himself to an unlettered girl from a poor Indian family; a Western skeptic won over to faith by the power and spiritual presence of an Eastern woman. Harvey's book had convincingly recorded his personal transformation, during which he reached great heights of ecstatic love and devotion for Meera, his master.

I loved the idea of an Oxford scholar swept by mystical passion. The day we came back from Point Reyes I immediately called Gaia Books, a spiritual bookstore in Berkeley, to get my own copy of *The Hidden Journey*. The salesman mentioned that Andrew Harvey would be speaking there the next evening. This seemed a wondrous "coincidence." I was determined to go, even after a full day of clients. Renate, who works late on Tuesdays, decided to meet me there toward the end of Harvey's talk.

She had by now read much of *Hidden Journey* and didn't like its author. She felt him to be melodramatic, self-involved. I was captivated by his intensity, which reminded me of myself. But, he experienced elaborate, dramatic visions, while I feel and see mystically as I move through the ordinary world, the light breaking into golden radiance while I am standing at the stove stirring a pot of vegetable soup.

The man on the telephone told me the tickets would cost more than usual because the reading was a benefit for Andrew Harvey.

"Oh, a benefit," I said. "Is he doing work on behalf of Mother Meera?"

"Actually, he's had a little falling out with Mother Meera."

"A little falling out with the divine mother?"

"He'll probably speak about it," my informant said.

Master and disciple—a passionate, turbulent, fiery lineage. I should not have been surprised to hear of a break between Meera and her devotee. "Ah, yes," says the Zen archery master, "I have taught my students and now their arrows are turned against me." Nevertheless, I felt suddenly anxious, as if I might hear something devastating from Harvey that would interfere with my conviction that I had something essential to learn from Mother Meera about my service to the world.

When had I developed this conviction?

I arrived early for the Harvey talk, browsed about looking for books about Mother Meera, which were hidden away behind the shelves moved to accommodate the audience. I kept reaching through the narrow space between shelves, but didn't get anywhere. Instead, I found a book about women saints of India, the other "mothers" who are worshiped in India as divine and are also called affectionately, and with devotion, "Ma."

I was happy to know Meera belonged to a cultural form of which I had been ignorant, in which women saints are worshiped as deities who become incarnate to bring love, memory, a divine message, perform a healing task, repair and perhaps save the world. This was, I thought, the Hindu version of the Shekinah. Wonderful, that it had not died out or disappeared or fallen into (merely) legend. If I had been born and raised in India I might have felt right at home with people who recognize divinity in human beings. Perhaps I would have been like Mr. Reddy or Adilakshmi, an educated person from a privileged life, who could nevertheless set out looking for the divine mother with a traditional sense that such quests made sense within their culture.

I know many people who are fascinated by the concept of the Shekinah, who name and celebrate her symbolic presence and passage through the Sabbath. None of them thinks of her as living a quiet life in an obscure German village, where she avoids publicity, does her own plumbing, loves to garden, builds her own house, is less than five feet tall, never charges for the spiritual help she gives strangers and devotees alike.

So here I sit, inwardly very excited because I am about to meet up with a man who has known the mother, worked with her, worshiped her, been transformed by her; at the same time, I'm agitated at the way he's been able to break with her and worried about what kind of person he might be. Although he never describes himself in the book, I have imagined an exceptionally beautiful young boy, more Indian than English, with large, dark eyes.

The audience is younger than I expected, composed of equal numbers of men and women. I have the impression belief has come easier to them, they haven't had to struggle as hard as I to overcome their cynicism, their skepticism, their logical quibbles. But what do I know? Maybe I look calm and serene to them too.

Then I notice that my father is sitting beside me. He seems surprised to find himself in this room filled with spiritual books. He looks questioningly at me. Has he been resurrected after all in a believer's heaven? In his presence I feel particularly Jewish, intense, brooding, full of struggle and doubt, not at all a New Age personality. I feel old, as if I were one of those old souls people talk about, who has seen everything, lived everything, known everything. I wish the reading would begin.

Harvey shows up, an engaging man in his early forties, with an arresting, proud, sensitive face. He clowns around some, seems at ease, speaks with a rapid-fire brilliance that is immediately compelling, reads his own translations of Rumi's sacred love songs, tells parables eloquently, in a resonant upper-class English voice. He has a charismatic presence, you can't take your eyes off him, yet he seems to be a man whose heart is breaking. Other people clearly do not feel this way. Many have their eyes closed, are swaying and nodding; others listen with rapt concentration, laughing readily at his jokes. From what he says and doesn't say (he never mentions Mother Meera) I begin to wonder if he has perhaps broken with her over a question of sexuality. He gives me the impression of a man who has recently lost himself. If this is what work with Mother Meera has brought him maybe she isn't what I've begun to hope she might be.

During the question period I try to ask about his break with Mother Meera. He doesn't call on me, perhaps because I have been visibly disturbed through the entire presentation. Renate shows up. The minute I catch sight of her my father is no longer present. Her skepticism replaces his.

I go to sit with her in the back of the room. She wonders if Harvey is the sort of person always talking about transformation who is never changed.

"What if the same thing is true of me too?" I whisper.

We are walking out to the parking lot. We run to get

across the street. She grabs my hand, I run faster, then she gets ahead. We are wondering why Renate is not interested in him while I find him fascinating. Have I found in Andrew Harvey a shadow version of my self, the shadowy eternal seeker? Meanwhile, we stand face to face next to her car, a cold, dreadful suspense blowing up around us as we try to figure out who we are, where we are going, whether we are going on together.

I REMIND MYSELF: my interest in the spiritual grew while Lynn was dying. I acknowledge: this could mean, in my desperation about not knowing how to help her, I invented a soothing fiction. A spiritual world. It could also mean that her dying and my response to it threw open doors of perception that had always almost been open, then never quite, then widely thrown open, then banged shut.

Coincidence or significant occurrence? Taken merely as facts, there is nothing to debate: Lynn is dying, I am given a book, a dormant spiritual interest awakens, Andrew Harvey reads in Berkeley. A few days later my old friend Dov shows up on a business trip.

I drive across the bridge to San Francisco to see Dov.

When he walks into the hotel lobby it occurs to me that he too is a brilliant intellectual who has devoted his life to a spiritual practice. But he has been changed by it.

We have lunch at Green's, at a table over the water, shyly staring out at the Golden Gate Bridge. It takes time before we find each other. I have waffles with fresh fruit, he eats a pita sandwich. We both drink decaf espresso. Then we walk through Crissy Field, out along the bay toward the bridge. A wind comes up. He offers me his arm. We might be back in Acco, or on the kibbutz where we met, walking at the edge of the farm when he was still a soldier. We walk through the wind, in a very bright sun, arm in arm, comrades. Our passion of twenty-two years ago follows far behind us. I have been telling him about Mother Meera and Andrew Harvey.

"What happens in the heart matters," he says, his hand lightly touching his chest. "Nothing else."

When I tell him that Meera is the first spiritual teacher I have ever wanted to visit, he stops walking, turns to face me. "You must go, even if you are disappointed you must go and it will have been worthwhile. Really, you must do it."

"And Renate? What if she doesn't want to come?"

"That's serious. If only one person in a couple is in love with the divine . . ." He looks worried and I'm scared.

"Say it, I want to know what you think." Then, because he hesitates, "I'm not afraid."

"The love for the divine is very passionate," he says hesitantly. "If two do not feel it together, if they are not brought together through this shared love, there might be trouble."

In that moment I know that I am going to do it. I am going to visit Meera. A direction has been established, a path leads in that direction, Mother Meera is on this path, even if she is not the guide/hope/teacher I want her to be. I say this more ecstatically than I had intended, egged on by the wind, the closeness of this man I once loved passionately, by a strange, haunted gratitude for whatever has brought us back together, right now, after so many years.

None of this seems strange to Dov, who has been studying and meditating for the last twenty years. He is sitting next to me on the bench watching an old woman walk her dogs. In his presence, everything spiritual seems matter-of-fact, familiar.

Some people have teachers, he says. Others follow a path with an unknown guide, as if the guide were walking ahead of you through the sand. The light is so bright you can't see him. He is wearing a cloak that wipes away his footprints in the sand. When you look behind you, there are only your footprints. Nevertheless you know for certain you are being guided.

The wind is blowing his hair back off his forehead, uncovering his face. "You look like the Dov of long ago."

"Maybe it's the conversation we are having."

"Out of all those people I knew on the kibbutz you and I are the only two still in a relationship with each other. Is it because we are on the same path?"

"Of course," he says.

Arm in arm, hand in hand, both of us careful; nothing erotic is allowed to enter this bond. It seems to have grown into a spiritual comradeship. Perhaps that is what we were after years ago when we lay on my small bed reading and debating.

How carefully he kisses me on the cheek when we say good-bye at his hotel. It will be years before I see him again, he won't write. But if I want to come to England, on my way to visit Mother Meera, I have an invitation from him and his wife.

Driving home, I feel as if I'm being plowed up and

turned over inwardly, made into someone else before my very eyes, or made more of myself, of what I was intended to be, whatever that means. If I had been a little girl in India, instead of a red-diaper baby in the Bronx, I would surely have one day taken off to look for an incarnation of the divine.

MARXIST MATERIALISM TRAINS a very precise, skeptical mind. With a mind of this type it would not be easy to wander about in search of a god. My own mind—shaped since childhood in a Marxist household—seems just as it has always been, precise, skeptical. But something seems to have unhooked it from these "other" experiences, which go right on happening no matter what I say or think about them. The precise, skeptical mind no longer has the power to keep them out, or away, or diminish them, by calling them nonsense.

I was in my kitchen the other day when I observed a singular, suspended, incandescent point of light at the edge of a glass jar filled with pebbles. Ah, there she goes again, I was about to say, when I noticed that the light had begun to expand, gather fullness, visibly ripen before my eyes. I remained in a state of ordinary mindedness, in the presence of things waiting to be done, as the dishwasher moved into another cycle and the bus gathered speed on the street outside the house. Nevertheless, I got the impression I was being offered knowledge, as if the things we need to know about the world come to us through moments so subtle they have moved on by the time we are aware that something, almost too fine for us, has been and gone.

Maybe mind fundamentally cannot grasp the ways of the heart. And no reason that it should. It has enough to do, precision instrument that it is, clocking, measuring, creating its world of plausible separations, reliable categories. If it could only learn to leave the heart alone, unfettered, in its playful mysteries.

The divine is not quite loud enough for us, not sufficiently garish to attract our notice. It moves with muffled footsteps in and out of the very world we inhabit, leaving traces of subtle disorder, a fine brushwork of disappearing acts for us to dust away as we go about to set our house in order.

Renate thinks I allowed myself to be fascinated by these muffled steps since I walked out of psychoanalysis. There, I was always accounting for things, busily making psyche out of ecstatic experiences, studying mind through them, the so-called altered states, the unconscious, the magical mind of childhood. All rot. I'm sick of accounting for mystical states. I'm just going to let them happen, the more I'm down on my knees the better. Perhaps this is what is meant by surrender. Perhaps surrender is what happened in the garden, at Abbott's Lagoon, on our walks through the woods, suddenly, after all those tedious years of making accounts.

The night after I left psychoanalysis I had a dream in which a man, a stranger, was showing me the way on Mount Tamalpais. I knew the regular paths very well, having gone there practically every Sunday with David, my husband, when I was in my early twenties. But this new guide knew subtle, mysterious, hidden connections between the known paths. I wrote the dream down, with a marginal comment: "I've ended psychoanalysis. I guess I've found a new guide."

That was in March 1992, two years before I write this account.

I leave psychoanalysis. I acquire a dream guide. I stand on a ladder in the garden. I am given a book. I go for a walk. Dov comes to visit. Light begins to look like wisdom. I can't stop thinking about Mother Meera. Patching it all together, a pattern emerges.

Sometimes I think that the people who have come to work with me, especially during the last few years, have been "sent" to me. Preposterous.

What sort of mechanism would patiently match up clients with their appropriate listeners?

But what if the idea hints at a world in which people of like mind are brought together to accomplish essential work that may make them useful to the world? Perhaps when people begin to awaken, grow sensitive, get a hankering for the divine, they give off a faint charge, rather like a remote radio signal, which is sensed or detected by other people similarly waking up? When my clients think these things I tend to be on guard, keeping an eye out for evidence of psychotic thinking. But the idea itself is not evidence of psychosis.

Certainly, during the last years, my work with clients has undergone a transformation. I listen to them with a question mark around my own comments and questions. Fixed boundaries begin to shift and yield. People are encouraged to stand at the door excitedly telling me something before they leave. (There are some things that can only be spoken with one foot out the door.) I welcome the messages that come in by fax from a woman who cannot yet say what is essential to her while she is in the room with me. The atmosphere of my consultation has changed. We are now comrades, allies, fellow conspirators working together.

Suddenly, it has occurred to me that this work of self-knowing has led most people I have spoken with over the years directly back into the world. Here, right in my consultation room, I have had abundant evidence that soul-work, this private, seemingly solipsistic absorption in the minutiae of the self, arrives sooner or later at a sense of vocation, of mission. I have clients and former clients who have been taking on local school boards to get adequate care for vulnerable kids, fighting to save the wetlands, bringing innovative programs into mental hospitals, developing community watch groups to monitor the public mistreatment of children. Our work, which has begun in the deep psychological realm, has gone on to include the experience of obscure spiritual yearnings. These have led to an engaged relationship with the world. And all this while I myself remained unaware of the pattern.

These days, I can't wait for people to arrive to go on

with their story. They come in eagerly, they can't wait to get to the chair, to the couch, to settle down to work. Our work has become almost playful, with that serious, rapt concentration children direct toward sand castles, those forever-inscribed soul monuments to the self's impermanence.

Have these elusive awakenings been settling in because I am requiring myself to entertain ideas I would formerly have driven away in ridicule? Are they taking root because I am willing to take seriously moods and inclinations, whims and spontaneities I would have shrugged away? Perhaps there is no great mystery in all this, but rather a noticing of small, infinitely natural things that happen constantly, little beckonings, sudden bursts of light, odd, jagged moments of sensing, of knowing, which one must stop to take in, weigh seriously, so that they can grow in one and have their effect. What have I done during the last weeks since I read about Mother Meera? I have started paying attention.

God died, that's for sure, but seems to have at least as many lives as a cat. How many times I've tossed the whole thing out (tossed out the divine!) to find that it always lands on its feet again, yellow-eyed, stalking me.

YES, I SEE: by writing, I have driven into the foreground these wispy, spiritual oddities that are usually swept into corners. By taking the ineffable seriously enough to write it down, I have made it more concrete. The quickly-passing, the almost-there, along with the shrugged-off, the evaded, have become the center of my work. With this move from periphery to center, spiritual matters have become the organizing principle of my life.

If only it lasts!

Meanwhile, Renate and I are on our way out to Point Reyes. I am driving. I take my hands off the wheel to tell her about my yearning for an act that expresses the deep-rooted stability of these transformations. I require a gesture that overcomes the perennial cycles of falling away, forgetting. A now or never urgency lashes through the early summer day. It is an odd wrenching, as of someone trying to tear me away from Renate.

That means I cannot trust to silence. I will talk, words will be pressed into a task impossible for them. They will try to cross the conceptual divide that is, I fear, growing up between us.

Transformation has to mean engagement, connection, common purpose. It cannot be the force that tears me away, alienates me from my surroundings, sets me off alone, isolates and removes me from the world. It must be possible to love the human and seek the divine, to be deeply attached to the earth and all its entanglements and still be trotting along on a spiritual course.

In a rush then, I say to Renate, who has been gazing into the trees, how deeply I have always been fascinated by silence, by whatever can be communicated without words, purely through presence.

"I see, you love silence," she says, with that tender irony I like for its capacity to take me seriously and to rebuke me.

"Well, yes. But still. Sometimes things have to be said or you never know what the other person might be thinking."

Renate reminds me to look at the road. I can't read her face, which seems sober, almost stern, as if she anticipates the tirade that is coming, while at the same time there is a suggestion of a smile, something she is holding back, waiting to tell me.

And now I'm off: I am drawn to the absence of dogma, I say, fascinated by the wildly daring openness of what Meera offers, this venture, in which you become yourself or more of yourself or nothing happens and Meera goes on, silently responding to the people who come to her. Without a doubt, she is living out a rare degree of belief in herself, both in her life as a woman and in her capacity to carry the burden of self-knowledge as divine. To give everything you have to another person, tirelessly, day after day, to complete strangers, without expecting anything in return, seems to me so rare, so remarkable I want to know more about it. To have so much to give is itself divine, I say, with a rising pitch to my voice. But I know that here I have gone too far.

That means I will now say more, I will talk faster, grow uneasy about Renate's silence, although I am leaving no room for her to say a word.

This young woman, Meera, a good twenty years younger than I am, possesses a confidence that allows her to walk into a room filled with people who expect everything in the world from her, to face them in perfect, unbroken concentration while the room becomes irradiated with light because she sits there. I love all this, I love its challenge, its simplicity, its great good humor. She arrives in a culture where god has been declared dead. She builds her own home on the outskirts of an obscure German village. People begin to speak of a divine presence living among them. The very idea, at first ludicrous, absurd, dismissible, gradually undermines one's secular assumptions. Here we are, a culture for whom god has died, in which we have given up the possibility of knowing truth. In this poignant moment a small, dark-skinned woman has come among us in the belief that the world is under divine protection and that she is divine. Now we are compelled to question our basic assumption that god is dead. If we know nothing for certain we cannot know this. The scientific arrogance, the trust in the rational powers of the mind, the secular humanist pride that we can manage on our own have fallen before the threatened collapse of our civilization. I am dazzled that such a thing as a divine messenger might exist, someone who knows how to instruct a soul-seeker, as a piano teacher might guide a promising student or a voice teacher help to create a trained voice.

Renate has been reassured about me lately because I hadn't charged off to Germany to visit Meera the day after I heard about her. She had been impressed with my ability to stop talking about Meera whenever I detected signs of fatigue in my listener. She liked the way I weighed favorable and unfavorable reports dispassionately. But why a teacher? We'd been tottering along on a vaguely defined spiritual course for years together, as we now understood from our conversations and confessions.

Why a teacher?

We get out of the car, lie down under the trees, pick up some pine needles. I crush them for the smell.

"Okay," I say. "Okay, here's how it goes. We know nothing about the divine, right? We do not even know if the divine exists. Yet we are absolutely sure that if it did exist it could not possibly embody itself."

Renate puts her arms around me the way we do when we think one of us is about to cry. My voice is muffled against her breast.

"But don't you see? Gods and spirits might be walking all over this earth at every moment, only we are too busy to notice. None of this has to be true, it just has to be possible. In that possibility, merely in the possibility, stands a whole new life. But of course, to decide for oneself if something is possible one would have to experience it. One couldn't take the experience of anyone else, or a culture's prejudice for or against the experience. One would simply have to throw oneself open to the experience and then decide."

"It sounds like you're planning a trip to Germany."

"It sounds like you're not planning to come with me."

"I wouldn't be so sure."

Sometimes, in California, if you are lying in the woods in the early morning, you can watch the mist rise straight up off the trees. Suddenly the patchwork of sky comes through; then, if you're in a good mood, you feel as if you are participating in the creation of the world.

"You remember that dream I had that you had gone off to visit a woman spiritual teacher?" Her quiet voice is booming through the woodland silence. "I had another dream last night. We were staying somewhere in a large house. I woke up, you weren't there, I wondered where you had gone, and then I thought to myself, I too want to see the avatars."

Renate likes to introduce suspense into her stories. Just when you least expect it she stops to take a breath, then doesn't go on.

Well, you say, so what happens then?

Well, she will respond, just listen.

"I knew there were three avatars who were staying right in the neighborhood of our house. I went over, it was evening, and looked into the window. These were German houses and German windows, simple, solid. I thought I saw something in the upper window. I threw a couple of pebbles up as a code. It was a good idea. Suddenly there were three children in the window, looking down as curiously as I was looking up. They all had dark skin and hair and eyes. They looked Indian or Asian, it wasn't possible to be sure, although I could see them more and more clearly. I was enchanted by their presence, as they were by mine. I threw them a kiss, I had to do something to give expression to what I was feeling. Now suddenly the joy in the room up there grew to a roar. I heard something like shouting and jubilation and felt like a fool, throwing kisses to the avatars. Suddenly it was still, the little heads disappeared. Undoubtedly the parents had come in to quiet things down. But I heard the children singing: "*Shalom, shalom,*" they sang and then other words in an unfamiliar language.

"I went home, opened the door, and heard the same beautiful song filling the house. It came from above, from your room, and you were singing along with it, a bit shyly and almost on key.

"Is that singing coming from a radio? I wondered. But I knew that it was not coming from a radio.

"It's a transmission, I thought, and felt amazed to find the avatar children in our own house."

While Renate speaks, I have been lying with my head on her shoulder. The whole time she is telling me the dream I think, Now we'll know, now it will be decided. Either I go on alone or we'll go together.

I have a moment of excruciating fear when the dream-Renate feels like a fool. But now it is alright. Fools or not, we are going to Germany. What we find there is unimportant. What matters is the decision to have a look. We have crossed a conceptual barrier. If we have to go halfway across the world to find out whether a young Hindu woman has something to teach us, we are going.

We are on the same path. We are going together.

I see clearly how the last months have been folded together. My father's "return," Lynn's death, the grandchild who has been given to me, my impulse to break free of all tepid, "reasonable" thought. These together with Mother Meera are a single tuck.

Sometimes, during the last days, I have felt like one of the three Magi, setting out to look for god. It always must have been a question of rumor and story, setting off with precious gifts, knowing there will be nothing to guide you, unless the old stories prove true. For other people the infant asleep in the cowshed will be just another homeless person. For you, the possibility, after all those years of wandering and despair, that this time you will have found your god.

There is no way to temper the hope I feel, having crossed over into a conceptual world where a venture of this type (admittedly, against the odds) seems worth undertaking. If the divine exists, why shouldn't it be able to manifest itself? If it can manifest itself, why not as a young Hindu woman who lives in Germany? If this woman, why not visit her? But if one is to visit her, why not with a state of mind in which nothing is known for sure, either proved or disproved, in which therefore anything is possible?

This is not faith. (Faith knows, faith believes.) This is the wild night, the sudden radical suspension of disbelief in the name of possibility.

WE HAVE MUCH to talk over, my father and I. There are the loose threads to catch up, stories that have evolved further, events that have emerged to fulfill a pattern. We are out for a walk, up in the woods above my house, the place where I once walked with my mother when I was writing a book about her life. The bench we sat on then, near the pond, has been submerged. There is no trace of it left, although I know the spot where it once stood, before the rains came. Even in an imaginary act there is a sense of time. Where there is time, time is always running out.

I want to tell my father about our visit to Mother Meera, although I know my father will find it inconceivable that his daughter has gone halfway across the world to receive the blessing of a divine mother. I could pretend I am fascinated by the personality of any woman who claims she is here to save the world. But I have traveled to Germany to find out for myself if Meera is divine. That is what I want to explain to my father.

Meera's house is at the edge of a small village called Thalheim, part of a network of villages connected by paths that cross fields in which kale is growing. It was winter when we arrived, some of the fields had been deeply furrowed, their rich, dark soil lying open under an enormous sky, where heavy clouds gather, threaten rain, disperse beneath angular shafts of sunlight. A river runs through the back garden of Meera's house, a modern, concrete building in a village with some beautiful old seventeenth- and eighteenth-century half-timber houses and barns. Andrew Harvey had described the villages as stuffy and provincial, not charmed, apparently, as we were by the slate roofs, the winding forest path that leads through poplar and pine woods past the stations of the cross to a sacred Celtic site on which there now stands an old stone church that looks down into the village of Frickhofen. There we stayed for ten days, rising late to eat an enormous German breakfast before we set out for our daily walk to Thalheim, to visit the grave where Mr. Reddy, Meera's uncle, who died in 1985, is buried.

On the four nights a week when Meera offers *darshan*, visitors gather in the parking lot at the edge of Thalheim. These arrangements have become necessary because Meera does not want the villagers disturbed by her visitors. Silently, then, in groups of fifteen or twenty, we walk, sometimes through the rain, to Meera's house on the far side of the village. We are pilgrims who have come far to reach a distant shrine. I feel strangely giddy at this idea, as if I had traveled backward in time and not merely across the world.

The room in which Meera receives visitors is no longer large enough for the numbers of people who wish to come. Many people have to sit in the back, or in adjacent rooms, where they are not able to see Meera until they come forward to receive *darshan*. We had been lucky on our first night and were given seats along the wall directly in front of the low white chair in which Meera will sit. The austere room, cold at first, filled up slowly. People had to stop in the narrow corridor to remove their coats and shoes. They entered one at a time, were greeted silently by Adilakshmi, who directed them to vacant chairs or indicated places on the floor where they could sit.

We had not slept the night before during our plane ride. Renate was exhausted. She whispered to me, as the room began to grow hot and stuffy, that she would probably go out and lie down in the car. I was not to worry about her, I could stay as long as I liked, she'd sleep until *darshan* was over.

A few moments later Meera entered the room. We all stood, some people bowed their heads. The room was extravagantly quiet, as if simultaneously two hundred people had just caught their breath. Meera, with a slight rustle of silk, moved across the room as if she were a focused beam of energy, her small, quick steps giving an impression of purpose and humility.

As soon as she was seated Adilakshmi knelt in front of her. Meera put her hands on Adilakshmi's head and we now saw for the first time Meera's gaze of concentrated power, as if her entire being were present in her eyes, her compassion, her dedication, her freely giving of all she had to give.

By the time we sat down again, Renate was weeping.

I know Renate well, she would hate to weep in public. But from the moment Meera entered the room, Renate had perceived Meera's sense of mission and its immense, inhuman loneliness. Renate, the skeptic, who had been prepared to spend the evening asleep in the car, had been gripped by compassion for this tiny, childlike woman who had taken on the fate of the world.

I thought I had come to find out if Meera was divine. Was she divine? But how could I possibly know, having never knowingly encountered the divine before?

Certainly she was extraordinary. I too was impressed with her sense of dedication, the sustained, unbroken concentration she directed toward the people who now began, one by one, to go forward, to kneel before her to receive her blessing.

Nadine had felt silence, Renate was weeping quietly, I

would have been laughing raucously if I had dared. I had come halfway across the world to find exactly what I knew would be there. Therefore, I had no way of knowing if the woman I beheld possessed the extraordinary compassion I seemed to see in her, or was merely the inevitable confirmation of what I had expected to find. If I had been laughing as I went forward to receive her blessing, if I had dared to laugh, it would have been with the realization that it did not make any difference.

I have no idea what the divine is, or whether it is embodied in Mother Meera. But while I was in the room with her it seemed to me that a luminous quiet filled every possible inch of space with the certainty that life had meaning, we were not alone here on earth, our world could be saved, powers known and unknown were at work to accomplish this. I would go home and find the useful work, the small, patient tasks for which I was intended. Was Meera one of these powers? She was. As was every person in the room, yes, potentially divine, if we were willing to take on responsibility for the planet.

This understanding is what I have wanted to explain to my father.

My father and I are walking through a long, soft late October light. I observe the troubled beauty of this light, falling, I think, with an awareness of its own mortality. Although I have come here to speak with my father, we are silent as we walk. There are small things scurrying in the bushes, a fallen tree rides out into the water, which has turned gloomy as the sun moves off. Far off, luminous ripples cross the pond, from no perceptible light source. My father will debate any issue with some of the keen concentration, some of the detachment with which he played chess, a game just serious enough to engage one's highest powers but a game nevertheless. He wonders if I have confused a beautiful, poetic idea with the truth. This is an opening move in a match he will conduct with decorum.

He knows as well as I Keats' famous identification of beauty with truth. But truth for my father must be clearly separated from poetry, certainly in relation to political acts. Have I come here to tell him that in the absence of any absolute standard for truth, a poetic sensibility may be our only guide?

He smiles thoughtfully at this idea as he stoops down to pick up a pinecone smeared with a sticky, amber sap.

We both gaze at it as he holds it up to the light, turning it slowly to release its viscous luminosity.

Suddenly, I want to talk to him about something bitter, silenced for a long time, about a child with an inborn spiritual inclination that was ignored, neglected, perhaps even shamed and ridiculed in our atheist household. I was taught to give up a world of magical surmisings that may, after all, be knowledge of our divine capacity to seize and serve the world. Fifty years later, I am still angry because I was taught to believe in the eternal opposition between spiritual hankerings and political acts.

My father's influence on me has always been transmitted through silence. Words have never been necessary for him. In this way he reminds me of Mother Meera, who speaks not one word to the people who come to her. But I have notions I am eager to share with my father. I want to tell him that a spiritual awakening may be the most revolutionary experience possible in our time, comparable in its power to motivate action as were the ideas, in their time, that workers and peasants could throw off exploitation and injustice.

My father and I sit side by side on neighboring tree stumps at the edge of the pond. When he observes the world, things that to me seem solid have a tendency to dissolve in patterns of light and shadow. The demanding beauty of this place, which makes it hard for me to sit still, quiets down when he looks at it, indifferent to the distinction I feel compelled to make between tree, sky, bird in passage overhead and their rippling, watery reflections. I have wanted to tell him that Marcie will give birth in three weeks. Everything about the pregnancy has gone well, miraculously so, I think, after all those years of struggle for conception. The other day I received a card from her with precise instructions for the drive to Sacramento, the exit I will take, the right turn on H Street to the hospital, the location of the parking lot, the maternity ward on the third floor. But talk seems unnecessary. He seems to know what there is to know, as if I have accepted him permanently as the witness to what I learn, set down, discover. "Every birth is a miracle," my father would say if he said anything, but silence is better.

My father has always known how easily thoughts flow from one person to another. But never before have I appreciated the gentleness of his thinking. He has understood, as my mother never could, the dilemma of a person who no longer believes in anything. For such a person the possibility of divine intervention, a hope hard won at the edge of complete indifference, may unlock the shattered capacity to take on the world.

My father muses, considering the odd possibility that it no longer matters whether or not an idea is true, so long as it restores connections, returns one to a sense of immediacy and concern and makes it possible then to act in a world threatened by disintegration.

This notion is strange to him. It causes him to stroke his mustache, his gaze fixed hard on the far side of the lake, where an egret has just emerged from the branches of a fallen tree to become visible near the water. The word "compassion," which did not exist in his vocabulary, sounds strange on my father's lips. Yet now he is being asked to consider whether a sense of compassion is perhaps in our time a revolutionary power. Very softly, almost inaudibly, I hear him take up the two words— "compassion," "revolution"—as if he were weighing them to see how they might balance.

I wonder what my father knows about the world during the twenty-seven years he has been dead. Has he observed from far off the decline and fall of his own hopes and visions? If so, he may have come to understand Marxism as a cry of outrage against the nihilism of its time, a failed attempt to reawaken history on behalf of man.

Here, he would be thinking his way out of the reassurances of his own time into the bleakness of mine, trying to understand the state of mind in which people no longer believe in a future, so that the promise of a better society holds no promise for them.

If this thought proves possible for him, he will have understood why a fierce eruption of compassion may be needed before we can devote ourselves to the seemingly impossible task of saving our world. If there is no future, no systematic truth to guide us, no meaningful collaboration with historical forces, why act at all unless one cares violently, beyond all rational calculation, for life itself?

When we walk on, my father draws a shadow around himself, as if politely stepping aside. Strangely, there is no heartbreak, no wrenching disloyalty to the past, simply now, as I turn to look at him, a man who gardened as if he were at prayer, a matter of walking on into a dimension the family did not explore. When time runs out it does so without warning. Here, by the lake, a few feet behind us now, as we head for the hill where dried thistles stand, my father and I take leave of each other. If there had been time, I would have told him about the man dying of AIDS with whom I have begun, during the last weeks, awkwardly, tentatively, to talk about spiritual things. I have wanted to show my father the flocks of Canada geese that have been wintering during the last years in the pastures out by the reservoir. When you first come upon them, around the curve in the path, they seem a scattering of huge stones on the grass dunes where cows are grazing. Now I am running back, around the lake, to the dark side, which always seems dangerous after dusk, as if I were racing after him, wondering how I could have let him go, the story incomplete on the eve of departure.